The Best of
From Our Own
Correspondent

‹ 5 ›

Dec 94

Alan —
Best wishes this
Xmas
love from,

Susan + Karen.

BBC

The Best of
From Our Own
Correspondent
‹ 5 ›

Edited by
Tony Grant

Foreword by
John Simpson

I.B. Tauris Publishers
LONDON · NEW YORK

Published in 1994 by
I.B.Tauris & Co Ltd
45 Bloomsbury Square
London WC1A 2HY

175 Fifth Avenue
New York NY 10010

In the United States of America and Canada
distributed by
St Martin's Press
175 Fifth Avenue
New York
NY 10010

The text of this book is drawn from original material
broadcast by the BBC News and Current Affairs and the
BBC World Service Directorates.

'BBC' and the BBC logotypes are trademarks of the British
Broadcasting Corporation and are used under licence.

A full CIP record for this book is available from the
British Library.

A full CIP record for this book is available from the
Library of Congress.

ISBN 1 85043 872 2

Set in Monotype Janson by Ewan Smith.
Printed and bound in Great Britain by
WBC Ltd, Bridgend, Mid Glamorgan.

CONTENTS

FOREWORD

Compared to the business of reporting for radio and television news bulletins, which is the foreign correspondent's bread and butter, working for *From Our Own Correspondent* is usually pure enjoyment. It offers the chance to let yourself go slightly, to explain some of the things you have been wanting to tell your audience but never quite had the scope or the opportunity. Sometimes it provides what Fleet Street used to call 'local colour': giving the audience an idea of what it was like to be somewhere or to experience something. Best of all, you are freed from the tight controls of news reporting, and are not obliged to clip your words into staccato bursts of densely packed information. This is the programme which, more than any other, enables you to be a little less the emotionless purveyor of objective fact and a little more yourself.

The year reflected in these reports has seen not only one of the most hopeful events of modern times, the remarkably peaceful elections in South Africa which provided an example of moderation and reconciliation for the rest of the world, but also war, disease and massacre on a worse scale than before. The sterile discussion of 'good' versus 'bad' news seems even less relevant this year than it usually is. Much that was good and much that was bad happened and was reported: end of story. The duty of the broadcasters is to explain something of why these things took place, and *From Our Own Correspondent* provides the perfect opportunity.

Yet for someone who has been an occasional contributor to the programme over the years, and a far more frequent listener to it, one of the chief pleasures of *From Our Own Correspondent* is to hear a little of the real (as opposed to the formal and professional) voice of the person behind the microphone. In that sense, I hope, the contributors to this latest volume of reports will continue to be, as they have always been, very much our own correspondents.

John Simpson

ACKNOWLEDGEMENTS

The editor would like to thank all the correspondents who contributed to this book, and all those at BBC Newsgathering who enabled them to do so. He is also grateful to Mike Popham at Bush House for his help and encouragement and to Geoff Spink, Graham Fawcett and Allan Little for their assistance with the manuscript. He is indebted to Emma Sinclair-Wilson from I.B.Tauris and to Clare Lockhart, the Production Assistant on *From Our Own Correspondent*, whose help with this project has been invaluable.

AFRICA

SHEPARD'S FUNERAL

FERGAL KEANE   MABOPANE   19 AUGUST 1993

Black township violence claimed more than seventeen thousand lives in the years leading up to South Africa's historic election of 1994. Often, hundreds of people would be killed each month. It seemed that the security situation was deteriorating rapidly, and few people were untouched by the violence.

Death came to my personal world this week. It took away Shepard Gopi in a matter of seconds. He was a gentle human being whom I knew mostly as a husky voice floating in the warm darkness of my backyard. Shepard was the boyfriend of Paulina, an equally gentle person, who has worked for the BBC for some ten years. He had a job in a large furniture store, had his own car and seemed to all of us to be a happy man, a man who looked to the future. He divided his time between my house and that of a friend in nearby Alexandra township. When I returned home last Friday night, I found Paulina sitting at the kitchen table weeping, my wife doing what she could to offer consolation.

The facts, as explained to me, were brutally simple: the previous night Shepard had gone to Alexandra to meet his friend. They went to a drinking club and talked for several hours. When Shepard came out, a group of gunmen surrounded him. One of the gang opened fire with an automatic rifle and shot Shepard ten times. On a street where the rubbish is piled in mounds, Shepard Gopi, Shepard of the laughing voice, died in a pool of his own blood. The following day his father arrived at my house, carrying his son's clothes and a few other personal belongings. This was how Paulina learned of her lover's death.

As she sat weeping at the kitchen table I felt at a loss as to what to say, how to console her. But Paulina knew, far better than I, that

3

this was a death without sense, without reason, without meaning. 'These are terrible times. Why are we killing each other?' she asked. The answer, of course, was one that most people wanted to shy away from, a truth that lurked in the darkness. It lay in recognizing that the humanity had drained out of a great many people, that for the young men who killed Shepard it was as easy to take his life away as it would have been to allow him to live.

The generation that produced Shepard's killers had grown up believing that violence should be their first resort. They had good teachers: policemen who shot first and asked questions later, secret police who tortured and murdered with impunity and distant political leaders who urged them to make their townships ungovernable, their schools into places of revolution. But while the grown-ups have decided it is time to talk, the generation they spawned have begun to lose themselves in fields of blood. I have encountered such wild-eyed young men on the streets of the townships time and time again in the past month.

They are the people who place burning tyres around the necks of their victims, they make up the gangs that enforce school boycotts and strikes, they are the people who have of late taken to digging up the corpses of their enemies and setting them alight. This final act of desecration encapsulates the brutalization, the nihilism which is eating its way into the social fabric of those townships where violence has become endemic.

Before I lose myself in despair, let me return to the short life of Shepard, or more particularly to his funeral. With four of Paulina's friends packed into the car we set off early for the black homeland of Bophutatswana, to the township of Mabopane where the funeral was to take place. It was a bright, warm morning and the journey north took us barely forty minutes. This was a township quite different from the ones I had spent so much time in recently. There was order and quiet, with no barricades and no prowling armoured vehicles. We followed a long line of buses and cars to the dusty graveyard, which rose out of the bush about a mile from the township. At the graveside, the family congregated under an awning which had been specially erected. Behind them were singers from one of the burial societies to which township residents pay a sum each month to secure a decent funeral for family members.

The wind came up from the east and sent clouds of dust from the open grave drifting over the mourners. We coughed and turned our faces away. Some women began to sing a lament, one of those old cries of pain that seem to rise out of the ground and fill every pocket of space. One by one we walked to the grave and took a handful of earth, which we cast down onto the coffin of poor dead Shepard. A notice handed around to mourners noted that he had been born in 1961, and shot dead thirty-two years later. As the diggers began to shovel earth down into the grave, I wept for Shepard and his family and for Paulina, but also for the burned and mutilated dead who had crowded my dreams after the last terrible month in the townships. As we walked away from the graveyard, the minister who had performed the burial service came up to me.

'Thank you for coming,' he said, 'thank you so much. You see,' he said, 'it is that love that is important.' Standing amid the streams of mourners, I held on to his words: knowing that in their simplicity, they spoke volumes about this country's amazing capacity for hope in the face of fear, brutality and so much loss.

BLOODSHED IN BURUNDI

MARK DOYLE   BUJUMBURA   28 OCTOBER 1993

> *Months before the world became aware of the massacres being carried out in Rwanda, widespread tribal killings were taking place in Burundi, the country immediately to the south. As in Rwanda, the killings arose from enmity between the Tutsi and Hutu tribes.*

The misuse of money is said to be the root of all evil. The misuse of multi-party democracy in Africa sometimes seems to be the root of all violence. Politics has just entered a multi-party phase in this small state at the southern tip of East Africa's Great Rift Valley, and the trouble has begun. On the first day of my assignment, a Zairean priest explained Burundian politics to me. 'Every few years,' he said, 'the tall peple kill the short people.' That has proved to be simplistic, but the definition will do to set the scene. The tall people are the minority Tutsis; the short, the majority Hutus.

In truth, it is often difficult for a foreigner to tell a Tutsi from Hutu, since there has been much intermarriage. However, tribal animosities have mixed with politics to keep tension high, and Burundi's first experiment in multi-party democracy has been short and bloody. Many advocates of majority rule thought it was too good to be true when the Hutu got their first taste of power after generations of feudal rule by the Tutsi. They said it was as if Nelson Mandela had been elected in South Africa without the years of violence that that country has suffered in order for it to be achieved. Of course, South Africa is an important place, an investment prospect, and its growing pains are watched by the Western world. Burundi is small and strategically insignificant, so no one took much notice when democracy seemed to triumph.

Reporters like myself only took a look when things went wrong –

6

and they have gone badly wrong. Last week's coup by part of the
army left the Hutu president and several of his ministers dead. It
unleashed a series of revenge attacks by Hutu on Tutsi, then vice
versa, and more than a quarter of a million people fled to neighbouring countries. Thousands have died. On a helicopter trip around
the country, I saw apocalyptic scenes: hundreds of farms and fields
were burning as tribal and political violence engulfed the country. It
wasn't just Tutsis versus Hutus. A number of the short people decided
to vote with the mainly tall people's political party, the one that lost
in the free elections, and when it came to revenge attacks, first by the
short people, some of their tribal kin were targeted as well. In a
hilltop village in the centre of the country to which thousands of
people had fled, more than one hundred women and children were
burnt alive in a missionary outhouse. The rest of the refugees who
climbed the steep mountain paths to the mission were camped, path-
etically, inside the flimsy perimeter netting of an abandoned tennis
court.

In a valley nearby, plumes of smoke rose from hundreds of fires
started by attackers and looters. In a small market town, nothing
moved except a herd of cows. Everyone had fled or been killed; human
bodies littered the ground. Whole areas near neighbouring Rwanda
are depopulated. One of the many lakes which fill the mountain
valleys of the border area can be crossed by canoe in about an hour.
On the Burundian side, two plastic-covered blue armchairs sat on the
lake shore, items that someone had decided against trying to take to
Rwanda. While mass killings continued in the countryside, a bizarre
scene was being played out in the capital. Since the coup and the
killing of the president, the legal government has taken refuge in the
French Embassy. Inside the embassy, cabinet meetings take place and
the Burundian government holds court. I obtained a meeting with the
prime minister by passing a note via a French gendarme. The legal
government, at least those members of it not killed in the coup, refuse
to give up their diplomatic refuge because they say their lives are in
danger.

The Tutsi-dominated army, meanwhile, has furiously distanced
itself from the coup. It says it has returned to barracks and arrested
the coup-makers, who were not representative of the main officer
corps. It seems clear that one of the reasons for this backtracking is
the situation in the countryside, where Tutsis are being killed in
large numbers. Many have been seeking a way out of the political

impasse, and a way of stopping the killing. The government, holed up in the French Embassy, says it can never trust the Tutsi-dominated army again. It has called for an international force to guarantee constitutional rule. A senior UN official arrived in Burundi yesterday, but given the organization's many commitments and financial limitations, it seems unlikely that any significant force will come to this – on a world scale – relatively insignificant country. It is not clear who is running Burundi, or whether its democratic experiment will continue. What is clear is that thousands of people have died.

APARTHEID PROROGUED

FERGAL KEANE   CAPE TOWN
23 DECEMBER 1993

The mockery of democracy that was the old South African parliament met for a final session in the shadow of Table Mountain. For its MPs an uncertain future lay ahead, as most of them would be voted out of office in the coming all-race general election.

It is Christmas in Cape Town in the last days of the white empire, and the party is in full swing. The streets are crammed with shoppers and the beaches crowded with glistening bodies. Outside the temperature is a pleasant thirty degrees, and the heat not too oppressive thanks to the strong breezes that rush in from the Atlantic, scattering hats and scooping parasols out of the hands of old women as they wander along the promenade at Seapoint.

It is as if all the tensions and fear of the past year have been suspended for one last great spree, before the arrival of black rule with its myriad uncertainties. The bars and restaurants of the city's new waterfront complex are crammed. Talk of politics is politely discouraged. From a seat at one of the outdoor cafés you can gaze down towards the forests of bluegum trees, almost to the back gardens of princely houses on the lower slopes. All this week white parliamentarians have been enjoying these views, many of them knowing that it is the last time they will be doing so at the taxpayer's expense. Inside the Victorian building, with its cool marbled corridors and leather benches, its hints of Westminster and gentlemen's clubs, there is an atmosphere akin to the final week at school, before the students leave to face the challenges and pitfalls of the future. MPs have spent the days packing up their books and files, some having decided to retire, others hoping against hope that they will be returned after next April's all-race election.

From the back-benches the future looks anything but rosy: the latest polls give the National Party around 20 per cent of the vote, a figure which, if translated into seats in parliament, would mean that a large proportion of the sitting MPs would have to find other careers. And yet it is a view more pleasant by far than the one from the other side of Table Mountain. For there, on acres of dusty scrubland, are the South African majority, crammed in boxlike houses of one or two rooms, sheltering under the tin roofs of shanty towns or, in many cases, struggling to wrap pieces of old plastic over branches so that a rough tent-like structure is created. You can see them on your way to and from the soon-to-be-renamed D.F. Malan airport, a grey smear of shacks along the side of the road, a world the white passer-by enters at his peril. There are high watchtowers situated at strategic points along the highway. This is the consequence of several stone-throwing attacks on white motorists. Soldiers now watch over the sullen inmates of Guguletu, Crossroads and Khayelitsha, their automatic weapons a warning to any youths who might think of hurling a projectile at the tourists flocking to the beaches and winelands of the Cape.

This non-white majority has been denied political rights and human dignity throughout the three and a half centuries of white hegemony in South Africa. For them the parliament, with its pomp-filled official opening, its black-robed speaker and be-medalled state president, was the place where the misery of apartheid was constructed. All the laws of separation were promulgated and debated here, white voices discussing the ruin of non-white lives.

The man regarded as the true architect of apartheid, Hendrik Verwoerd, was assassinated in the same chamber in 1966. He was stabbed to death by a deranged messenger, who claimed that a tapeworm had told him to kill the prime minister. There were lone voices of protest like that of Helen Suzman, who used the parliamentary system to expose the lies and hypocrisy of successive governments. Other liberals followed in her wake, but there were no black voices to be heard, ever. They could enter this world only as servants, never as the political equals of the white overlords. In a few years' time people may well look back and shake their heads in amazement at the fact that in the latter part of the twentieth century a country existed where men and women were denied the right to vote because of the colour of their skin. That country is disappearing, the mockery of democracy which the parliament represented is fast becoming a memory, while the new lords of the future prepare to take over. They were in parliament this week. Watching from the public gallery was the ANC's Cyril Ramaphosa. Other members of his organization were being taken on tours of the building, some doubtless eyeing up the offices they will be occupying after next April. In the end the parliament the ANC once wanted to storm is being taken over by persuasion, and among many of the white MPs one detects a feeling of disbelief, as they gather their belongings and head out into the bright sunshine and uncertain future.

END OF THE RIGHT

TOM CARVER   MMABATHO   17 MARCH 1994

The threat to the future stability of South Africa posed by the militant white right receded sharply after an incident in the homeland of Bophutatswana.

To get to Bophutatswana you cross no physical boundaries, only barriers of the mind. The day we went there, there were no passport controls or sentry-boxes to mark our passage. We just drove for three hours west from Johannesburg through vast prairies of green maize eagerly soaking up the pure, uncluttered, early morning light. After a summer of rain, South Africa is promised a record harvest of food. In other parts of the continent that alone would have been sufficient to ensure happiness, but in South Africa life is never that simple.

Bophutatswana is, in fact, not one place but several separate states scattered across the map of South Africa as if thrown from an aircraft. Up until last week they had been held together not by any binding sense of unity but by the determination of the homeland's first and only president, Lucas Mangope. For seventeen years he ran the homeland like a personal fiefdom, untroubled by any thoughts of democracy.

The morning we arrived at the Mmabatho Sun, the main hotel in the capital, three days of continuous riots and strikes by the people had reduced much of the centre of the town to a wasteland. The main shopping arcade on Lucas Mangope Drive, once much loved by Bophutatswana's pampered elite, was no more than a smouldering ruin. In shops that had once stocked expensive European clothes, I saw through the broken glass only empty racks and used tear-gas canisters. The remains of a police armoured vehicle still burned outside the homeland's only university. At the entrance to the luxury hotel, we found seven mean-looking whites, with shotguns resting on their laps, sitting below a sign that advertised golf lessons. Inside, the place had been taken over by a siege mentality. The slot-machines and blackjack tables had all been closed. On the sun-deck an automatic pool-cleaner chugged along the bottom of the enormous pool like a caged animal, watched over by row upon row of empty deckchairs.

Only the cocktail bar was alive with activity. News photographers, dressed in battle fatigues and draped with cameras, lay sprawled on the plush sofas, whilst at the bar a small army of journalists drained the hotel's supply of soft drinks as their boots ground dirt into the well-padded carpets. Everyone felt they were witnessing an historical inevitability: the final death-throes of Bophutatswana in the face of democratic change. But no one had bargained on Lucas Mangope's last desperate gamble, an appeal to the right wing for help.

Into the cauldron of madness they came, an irregular army of farm pick-up trucks and cars with mud streaked down the sides. In the back, their legs dangling over the tailgates, sat bearded men with menacing looks, teenage sons proudly fondling their fathers' hunting rifles and mothers with pistols strapped to both hips. For several hours they cruised around the smoking remains of Mmabatho with the swagger of Hell's Angels. Everyone watched cautiously from the sidelines, uncertain what was going to happen next. I suspect that most of them on their pick-ups regarded it as a brave, even noble, adventure, like a medieval crusade. It was a sign of their political naivety that they were prepared to make a stand for a cause that was so clearly doomed – but at the time they seemed fearsome enough. This was the biggest display of right-wing solidarity yet seen, and it was clearly going to be a test of their resolve. As it turned out, it ended rather more quickly than anyone could have predicted.

A group of AWB (Afrikaner Weerstandsbeweging) men, travelling in a dilapidated green Mercedes, threw a racial taunt at a group of blacks. Suddenly sparked to anger, a member of the Bophutatswana police fired at the car, fatally wounding the driver. The other whites never saw it coming. They stumbled out of the vehicle, their hands in the air, suddenly no longer fearsome. But even then their arrogance let them down. One of them could not resist telling nearby journalists that the 'black bastards' didn't know what they were doing. Two minutes later, both men were dead, shot in the head by the policeman's colleagues. At that moment the myth of the right wing was shattered. In the chaos that followed, the policemen, suddenly panicking at what they had done, yelled at the watching journalists to get out of the area. But I could not take my eyes off the two AWB men dressed in their uniform of khaki shorts and shirts, with their pistols still in their holsters, lying face-down in pools of blood.

Two days later a photograph appeared on the front of South Africa's Sunday newspapers which must have turned the country's whites cold with shock. It showed the point of death: a black man in a uniform stood pointing a rifle down at the head of a white lying prostrate in the dirt. Such images have not been seen in Africa since Rhodesia and the days of the Belgian Congo. But in South Africa, shielded for so many years by apartheid, they have never been seen before. Optimists say that this incident will bring the right wing to its senses and finally make it realize that what it is playing at is no longer some brave game. Pessimists say that these were the first shots of a racial war. Either way, what happened in Bophutatswana has rocked a country already balancing on the edge.

WAR IN NATAL

FERGAL KEANE   PORT SHEPSTONE
7 APRIL 1994

As South Africans prepared to go to the polls, President de Klerk, faced with a mounting tide of violence, declared a state of emergency in Natal, in the east of the country. Fighting between supporters of the African National Congress and the Inkatha Freedom Movement was blamed for most of the killings. As always, it was the poor and dispossessed who suffered the most.

There can be few places more pleasant than Port Shepstone's beach-front on an Easter Sunday morning. The surf, the briny scent in the air, the collective joy of families playing in the sea and sand, combine to give the impression of great calm. If you walk the short distance to the town centre, the air of stillness is enhanced. Nothing much moves here on a Sunday. It is quiet and peaceful and blessed with the presence of endless sunshine.

But when I arrived there on Easter Sunday, it was not to enjoy the pleasures of the sea, or to soak in the relaxed colonial atmosphere. I had come in search of Natal's war, a war that lay beyond the white town among the hills and valleys further inland. There had been a massacre late the previous night: nine women and children murdered at a remote homestead in the Nkulu Valley. The details were sparse, but we did know that the dead were members of a family known to be sympathetic to the African National Congress. The man of the house, who was thought to be the main target of the attack, had escaped through a rear window and hidden in the bush. The local ANC office warned us not to venture into the area without guides, and so we duly waited outside the organization's headquarters in Port Shepstone until a car drew up, driven by the familiar figure of Cyril Shezi, a senior party official I had met before on previous visits to the area. In the past he had always come across as a rather diffident, quiet person. Now I thought I detected something close to raw fear on his face. A few weeks previously his direct senior, George Mbele, had been shot dead in front of a classroom full of schoolchildren. There were more than a few gunmen who wanted to kill Cyril, and he now travelled with a bodyguard who cradled a pump-action shotgun.

Cyril said he would take us as far as the police station closest to the Nkulu Valley. It would not be wise for him to go any further even with a bodyguard. The area was solidly Inkatha and Cyril's face was too well known for him to take a chance. The local police were friendly and would help, he assured me. We drove out of Port Shepstone and entered a landscape of tumbling hills and sugar-fields. The road dipped and rose away from the coast, pushing deeper into the tribal lands. 'Perfect ambush country,' one of my colleagues remarked as we came around a sharp bend overlooked by forested hills. I found myself slowing down, placing space between our car and that of Cyril and his driver. It was perhaps an ignoble response, but I did not want to become trapped in the crossfire should hidden gunmen decide to attack. After about fifteen minutes we reached the police station, where Cyril handed us over to the care of a black officer who told us to follow him along a rough mountain track. This was rutted with deep scars caused by soil erosion; small, conical huts clung to the hillsides and armies of goats munched the grass by the side of the track. Groups of women and children occasionally appeared, carrying water or huge bundles of sticks on their heads.

Then the soldiers appeared, suddenly jumping onto the roadway from their cover in a maize-field. With them was a young police lieutenant of Indian origin, who offered to take us to the scene of the massacre. We followed him across the field, encountering yet more troops crouched in among the tall maize plants, until we came to a collection of huts outside which stood a man and a young woman. The man's name was Ndazimbi Mzemelu, and he was a preacher. He agreed to talk and began to describe how the killers had come the night before and knocked on his door, demanding to see him.

One of the men outside the door had started shooting, and the people inside had tried to jump out of windows and escape. They were cut down with knives and axes as they ran. Mr Mzemelu described what had happened to his youngest child, a five-month-old girl. 'Baby was in her mother's arms, and the mother she dropped the child when she was hit with knives. The mother, my wife, she escaped and found the police. When we come back we found baby, but she was cut in the head really bad, and she died in the hospital.' He described this terrible scene in a quiet voice. Mr Mzemelu had lost his own mother and seven other members of his family in the attack. I formed the impression that he was talking to me from a place of deep shock, only vaguely aware of my presence and of my questions. Friends of the family had come and cleaned away the blood, but the bullet-holes and broken windows remained. Mr Mzemelu told me that the family had been warned to leave the area by Inkatha because one of his sons, who lived in distant Durban, was an ANC supporter. He had not left because he was a poor man, and if he left his land it would be taken over by other poor people.

That is the brutal and essential truth of Natal's war: it is a war of terrible cruelty fought among the dispossessed, a war which rarely, if ever, reaches the calm streets of Port Shepstone, but which becomes more fierce by the day. That there will be many more such massacres in the weeks ahead is the one prediction one can make with any certainty. This is the situation in Natal at a time when black South Africa should be looking to the elections with feelings of hopeful expectation. There is a madness spreading through the hinterland, a blood fever which could well turn the elections in the province into a civil war. A daughter of Mr Mzemelu's who survived the attack summed it up perfectly: 'I want to go and vote,' she said, 'but do you really think we can vote away the darkness in our hearts?' Unable to answer her question, I walked away from her towards the roadway.

RWANDA'S TRAGEDY

LINDSEY HILSUM NAIROBI 14 APRIL 1994

Lindsey Hilsum was working for an aid organization in Rwanda when the traditional animosity between the Hutus and Tutsis overflowed into violence and genocide. Within weeks, tens, possibly hundreds, of thousands of people had been killed.

The first weekend I was in Rwanda, an age ago at the beginning of February, Pasteur, one of the UNICEF drivers, took me to Byumba in the north of the country. He was nervous because there had been a lot of fighting in Byumba during the civil war. When we arrived he was surprised to see how calm it was, how life appeared to be getting back to normal, with people returning to their homes and planting their crops.

Pasteur is now dead, killed by a band of thugs who attacked the mission compound where he was hiding last weekend. Michel, another driver, is dead too, as well as Pauline, one of the secretaries, her husband and three-year-old child, and Serge, the doctor and all his seven children. I find it unbearable to associate these people with the anonymous bodies I've seen piled outside the hospital mortuary, machete wounds gaping, their faces frozen into blank stares. I'm not claiming that I knew these people well or loved them. But I had worked with them, and knew them as civilized people who, when I needed help because I was a foreigner in their country, gave it generously.

I am a journalist and sometimes an aid worker. My livelihood depends to some extent on the misfortunes of others. What responsibility does that give me? All through the week, I have been speaking to Rwandans I know – mainly people who work for UNICEF – by telephone. I have listened to their terrified voices recounting how soldiers killed their next-door neighbours then came to their own houses, threatened to kill them, took all their money and said they'd be back to carry out the threat. Then there are those whom I couldn't contact, whose phones went down, or who had no phone. What has happened to them?

I did nothing to help these people when they really needed help. By the time I left Rwanda, I had stopped ringing because I couldn't bear to hear the stories and have nothing to offer. I had no petrol in my car, I didn't really know where their houses were, and I had no money and no food. And I was too scared to go and find them, because I knew that if I tried to drive around town with Tutsis in my car I would become a target too. So I was useless.

The United Nations was useless, too. Senior UN staff begged for the rules to be bent, to allow for the evacuation of local staff as well as expatriates. The answer came back: 'No.' I know it would have been difficult – I know that getting foreigners out was complicated enough. But there is such a thing as responsibility, and maybe the UN peace-keeping force in Rwanda could have played a role by trying to evacuate Rwandans working for the UN and by intervening to try to stop the slaughter.

The United Nations has been active in trying to negotiate between rebels of the Rwandan Patriotic Front and the government troops, but most of the deaths of the past week have been caused by attacks on civilians by soldiers or armed thugs. The UN force was better armed than the Rwandan soldiers, but when the gendarmes and presidential guard refused to let the UN troops past road-blocks to the suburbs where the killings were going on, the UN gave in. When the slaughter was at its worst, the UN force was in its barracks. I know that if they had tried to storm their way through the road-blocks, then more UN soldiers would have been killed – but if a UN force is supposed to keep peace, how can it justify doing so little when the peace is brutally shattered, and when tens of thousands of people are being hacked to death in their houses and on the streets?

Since I left Kigali, I've been thinking about Oscar Schindler, the German who smuggled Jews out of Nazi Germany, whose name is now famous because of Steven Spielberg's film. I wonder if there are any Oscar Schindlers in Rwanda. I would like to think so. I would like to think that there was someone with the courage and the confidence it would take. If the institutions can't or won't do anything, the responsibility comes back to individuals.

Just as I was leaving Rwanda, I bumped into another secretary from UNICEF, who had managed to flee her home to somewhere slightly safer. I told her about Pasteur, Michel, Pauline and Serge. I regretted it, because it was the first news of her colleagues she had heard. She wept and clung to me and sobbed: 'Rwanda isn't a country any more, there's nothing to do but run as far away as possible and never come back.' Some will do that, of course, and hundreds of thousands of Rwandan refugees are expected to arrive in Burundi, Zaire and Tanzania. But most Rwandans will have no choice but to stay and live through the horror. Foreigners like me, of course, will be long gone, to the next country, with work to do and uneasy consciences to still.

THE LEGACY OF APARTHEID

TOM CARVER SOWETO 21 APRIL 1994

After years of suppression under the old regime, the blacks of South Africa had high hopes of the all-race election of April 1994 which had swept Nelson Mandela and the ANC to power. But it was clear that it would take years, if not decades, for the legacy of apartheid to be shaken off finally.

In his parents' home in Soweto, Mduduza Vilacase sits slumped in front of an old black-and-white television. The ancient device is hanging on to life only by the weakest of electrical connections; each time a lorry drives over the rutted track outside, the screen blanks out for a few seconds. The programme is a cheap daytime soap called *The Bold and Beautiful*, about rich families in California. It is intended for South Africa's bored white housewives, but Mduduza – black, male and twenty-six – can't take his eyes off it.

Mduduza is a typical Sowetan boy. When the 1976 riots began in the school just around the corner from his house, he was only eight. From that moment on his education effectively stopped – he went out onto the streets to throw stones uselessly at the armoured personnel carriers, while the army occupied his classrooms. By the time he was fifteen he was being regularly picked up and beaten by the police. At eighteen he made a run for it and disappeared into exile, spending six lonely years at various ANC camps in Angola and Tanzania before deciding it was safe to return in 1992. While Mduduza was in exile, the police would raid the family home demanding to know where he was. Sometimes they broke the door down, at other times they took his elderly parents away for questioning to the local police headquarters with anti-grenade shields on the windows.

21

If anyone should reap the rewards of change in South Africa it should be families like the Vilacases. They and hundreds of others like them fought to maintain their dignity as human beings throughout the years of humiliation that apartheid heaped on blacks – when they were strip-searched, when they had to step off the pavement to make way for a white. Families like them hid the picture of Mandela behind the calendar on the kitchen wall and dreamed about a better future.

But now that future is here they are discovering that nothing has really changed: the new South Africa is in danger of passing them by. They live in the same matchbox house they have been in since 1941, with eight people and one outside toilet. Mduduza spends every day in front of the TV because there are no jobs. He sacrificed his education to fight for his freedom, and has returned to find unemployment in Soweto running at 40 per cent.

You can feel the anger beginning to rise in him again. Every day he is reminded that it is the whites, the ones who grew fat on apartheid, who still carry home the spoils. It's the whites who have the automatic cars, the houses with swimming-pools, the jobs in the city. No one has taken any of that away from them – all that has happened is that a few of the luckier blacks have moved out of Soweto to join the whites in their leafy crime-free suburbs. The deepest scars of apartheid are those which no one can see. Apartheid has stripped South African blacks of virtually any sense of self-worth; it was designed so that blacks depended on whites for everything, especially work. They were allocated areas to live in but without the amenities, so roads weren't repaired, crime rose, and the rubbish mountains grew, while the white suburbs remained spotless.

Visitors to this country often say, rather peevishly, when they go to cities like Soweto that conditions are no worse than in the rest of Africa. That's true, of course, but what fewer people remember now is that much of South Africa's deprivation was caused by a deliberate policy. I look at Mduduza – a boy easily bright enough to have gone to university if he had ever had a chance to do so – and can see the anger consuming him inside. He feels humiliated that he cannot find a job to help out his parents, but as in the days when his stones rattled uselessly against the sides of the police armoured vehicles, his anger doesn't touch those it should.

So, as with so many black youths, his anger is turned in on himself, on his own family and friends. The psychological fallout of apartheid is destroying black life – tearing it apart like a dog with rabies. Johannesburg, and the townships which surround it, is one of the most dangerous areas on this planet, with unprecedented levels of domestic violence, crime and suicide.

As South Africa emerges blinking into the normal world after forty years trapped inside this deranged system, there are many good things to look forward to. For the first time youths like Mduduza will have a say in their country's destiny – ridding them, I hope, of their chronic sense of emasculation. But if anyone tells you apartheid is over, they are wrong. The legacy of this barbaric social experiment will haunt the majority of South Africa's population for years to come.

SOUTH AFRICA – MY HOME

NIGEL WRENCH   LICHTENBURG
28 APRIL 1994

Thousands of South Africans living far from home returned to their native land to vote in April's historic all-race elections. For some, it was a confusing experience.

Arriving in South Africa at Jan Smuts Airport used to be a reminder of how oppressive living here could be. You passed into the immigration hall guarded by armed policemen, a scowling clerk would flip through your passport (mine is British) and reluctantly, as if granting a favour, he would stamp it. When I returned last week, the experience could not have been more different. The policemen were gone, and the immigration clerk smiled and said, 'Welcome home, sir, welcome home.'

Like anyone with an uncertain nationality – I was born in Britain, but my parents emigrated to South Africa when I was a child – I have always had difficulty with the word 'home', even more so when it was applied to South Africa. How could a country that didn't allow most of its citizens the most basic of rights be home? How could a country that had detained some of my friends, and jailed some of my university lecturers, be home? And yet the smell of the dust after the rain, the colour of the jacarandas in the spring, the blue of the sky every morning, and the warmth of the welcome in the townships (when they were peaceful) were sometimes enough to overcome my reservations.

There was a certainty about apartheid: you hated the regime and loved aspects of the country. Now that's changed and, like many of my almost-countrymen, I have been left confused and disoriented. I have lived through any number of all-white South African elections. You always knew who was going to win – the National Party, whether led by John Vorster, P.W. Botha or F.W. de Klerk. Whites dutifully shooed them in; blacks were excluded as a matter of course. This time the National Party and the Liberal Democratic Party had their familiar posters on the lamp-posts on the drive from the airport into Johannesburg, but there too was the unthinkable – the black, green and gold of the African National Congress, arranged around the smiling face of Nelson Mandela.

I grew up in a South Africa where it was a crime even to possess a photograph of Nelson Mandela. At university we circulated illicit copies of his *No Easy Walk to Freedom* – just owning the lyrical book was enough to earn a prison sentence. As students we used illegally to type up pamphlets in Xhosa, a language none of us understood, demanding Mandela's freedom, and distribute them in the townships. I am sure now that those on the receiving end laughed at the grammar and spelling errors of these well-meaning 'whitey' students. Here suddenly, though, there were not only pictures of Mandela – pictures in newspapers and on state television, previously that most reviled of apartheid instruments – there was actually the opportunity to vote for him. I telephoned my mother, hoping for a little certainty. She last voted in 1970 for Edward Heath, just before we left Britain. Now a permanent resident in South Africa, she is allowed, for the first time, to vote in these elections. 'What do you think?' I asked. 'Well,' she said, 'I quite like Buthelezi.' I tried to talk her out of it. 'Wasn't Buthelezi responsible for massacres in Natal?' I asked. 'I like his smile,' she said, then she added, 'Maybe I'll vote for de Klerk. They say we whites should all stick together, so maybe I'll do that. The ANC are just communists.'

That was a phrase from the old South Africa: 'just communists'. It is a refrain that has again become familiar in the past ten days. A ruddy-faced white-haired man in a disturbingly tidy office in Pietersburg in the north fairly spat it at me: 'They're communists, and we won't have them ruling us,' he said. Erwen Haynes was the epitome of the sort of man I do not want as a fellow citizen – a good reason for not treating this country as home. But the difference this time is that the communists can answer back. At sunset in Tshing, a township outside Ventersdorp, the western Transvaal town where the far-right Afrikaner Resistance Movement has its headquarters, I met a young communist, Leshago Boikanyo – the head of the ANC there. He wore a South African Communist Party badge and a pair of fake Ray-Ban sunglasses. They have not had an easy time of it in Tshing. There have been several unexplained bomb blasts. The last, not four weeks ago, blew up a shack and injured the sleeping occupants. 'We're scared here at night,' said Leshago. 'So, what would you like to do to Eugene Terreblanche, the AWB leader?' I asked. 'We'd like to sit down and talk to him,' he replied, 'Mr Terreblanche needs people to give him direction.'

This communist threat seemed to me to be fairly benign, but maybe I was drunk on the South Africanness of the township sunset, the smoke from the cooking-fires against the orange of the setting sun. Those romantic symbols were once again getting the better of my judgement. The point about this confusing new South Africa is that it is meant to be confusing, filled with previously forbidden thoughts, people and pictures – and with changed and changing views. My sister-in-law could usually be relied on to say 'communist threat' about anything that was not the National Party. This, after all, was someone who had freely used the word 'coon' about anyone who wasn't white. When I last spoke to her, she was considering voting for Tokyo Sexwale, the leading ANC candidate – evidence enough that this country really is a changed place. I do not know yet whether my sister-in-law's nerve failed her when when she saw the ANC symbol on the ballot paper, and I do not know whether the voting experience was as profound for her as it was for me.

Yesterday afternoon, here in Lichtenburg, when the worst of the crowds had gone, I took a step towards being a real South African. I stood in line, had my identity document checked for validity, took a ballot paper and made my cross. I will leave you to guess who I voted for – it seemed the obvious choice. When I stepped out into the late afternoon sunshine, I felt as millions of black voters must have felt. I belonged to this place, this new South Africa – a South Africa that, finally, I am proud to call home.

THE NEW DAWN

FERGAL KEANE   JOHANNESBURG
30 APRIL 1994

The elections in South Africa, which brought more than three hundred years of white rule to a close, triggered reflections about the country's bloody past and its hopes for the future.

The past is a foreign country: they do things differently there. L.P. Hartley's glorious phrase seems perfectly apt on this soft autumn morning in the city of Johannesburg, in a South Africa which has vaulted away from its racist past into an unfamiliar era of hope. Rarely in the field of human experience can a nation so divided, so traumatized, have undergone so amazing a transformation. It is not that the racists of the far right have suddenly disappeared, or that the massive social inequalities have been removed. No, it's a deeper change by far. It is a change associated with the sweeping currents of the human spirit, and not with the the physical scars that have disfigured the face of this land for centuries. It is about the replacing of shame and humiliation with pride, about substituting guilt about the past with hope for the future.

When I first came here more than a decade ago, I recoiled at a country where people were forced to use separate rail carriages, toilets and beaches, because of their skin colour. The first rumours about the conflict that was to engulf the country and lead to several states of emergency were just beginning back then. The black trade unions were mobilizing, and the United Democratic Front – a coalition of anti-apartheid groups – was beginning the task of organizing nation-wide resistance to the government. But much as they protested, one never had the feeling that P.W. Botha and his government of securo-crats were about to be toppled. Under pressure they refined apartheid and abandoned many of its more obviously odious laws, but the bedrock premise that whites, and whites alone, knew what was good for blacks remained. Botha and his men were willing to bring blacks into government but only as junior partners, a jump up from their traditional role as servants and garden-boys, but only a marginal one.

I recall visiting Cape Town and mentioning the name of Nelson Mandela to some friends in a crowded restaurant. There were embarrassed glances, and somebody told me to keep quiet. Even mentioning the name of Mandela could draw the unwelcome attentions of the security police. Wandering back to my hotel that night I looked out across the great sweep of Table Bay to Robben Island. The lights of the island twinkled like frost against the dark Cape skies, and somewhere behind prison walls, hidden from the world, sat Nelson Mandela in the twenty-first year of his imprisonment.

Today he is sitting in the offices of the African National Congress in the centre of Johannesburg, just days away from being sworn in as the first black president of South Africa. Against every law of human nature, Nelson Mandela is appealing not for retribution against his jailers, against the people who subjected black South Africa to three centuries of shame, but for the opposite. Every public utterance of his within the past forty-eight hours has been directed towards the task of nation-building. 'The future belongs to all of us,' he is telling black, white, coloured and Indian South Africans. His main political opponent, F.W. de Klerk, the defeated candidate in strict voting terms, is anything but sullen and resentful. He too speaks of the need to put the past to one side and work together to deliver a country which can produce a better life for everyone. It won't be an easy task. The crushing burden of black expectations and the ever-present fears of whites will force the new government to walk a tightrope, giving enough to the majority to prevent political destabilization, but not taking away so much from the minority that they up and leave, taking their capital and assets with them. The problems of criminal violence will not suddenly disappear – only economic revitalization and a real improvement in people's living conditions can help end the spiral of murders and robberies. In the future, as over the past four years, the greatest burden of all will fall on the shoulders of Mandela and de Klerk. They face the challenge of living up to the rhetoric of nation-building, and to do this they will have to set aside the temptation to blame each other, when things – as they inevitably will – go wrong from time to time.

All that being said, I believe the new South Africa will be an infinitely better place than the old. It is difficult to measure in precise terms, because the elevation of the human spirit is not something one calculates in a mathematical way. Let me instead try to explain it with a brief snapshot taken from the countless images of the past few days that are running through my mind. I am standing outside a church hall in Soweto, it is tea-time and the darkness is coming on. Still there are lines of elderly people waiting to vote. An old man comes up and starts to talk. His face is lined and careworn, and I notice that he has a limp. This, he explains, is the result of torture at the hands of the security police during the Soweto riots of the mid-1970s. 'All that is long ago,' he says, 'we are wanting to put it behind us,' and then looking at me directly he utters a phrase I will always remember: 'Today, I became a human being.'

CAPE OF GOOD HOPE

JOHN SIMPSON CAPE TOWN 5 MAY 1994

The BBC's Foreign Affairs Editor was South Africa Correspondent in 1977–78, when apartheid was at its height. He returned to the country for the historic general election and found it a changed place.

The other day there was a service of thanksgiving in St George's Anglican Cathedral in Cape Town for the peaceful conclusion to the elections here. The congregation sang 'O God Our Help In Ages Past', with that slightly apologetic note in the voice that marks the influence of the English and their mild religious faith the world over. There were Indians and coloured people and Africans and whites there, and their words floated up to the groined roof of Sir Herbert Baker's incomparable piece of Edwardian Gothic. 'A thousand ages in thy sight, are like an evening gone,' they sang, 'Short as the watch that ends the night.'

It did indeed seem like just a few beats of recorded time since I'd been based here and watched the cruelty and wastefulness of the system that had now been swept away by the ever-rolling stream of history. In front of me in St George's were the rich stained glass and the delicately carved granite, but I scarcely noticed them. Other images were running through my mind instead: playing with my daughters on the beach at Cape Town on Christmas Day 1977 alongside all the other white families, while a row of black children sat on a low wall at the back of the beach, watching the enjoyment they were forbidden, by law, to share. I remembered our landlord showing us round the lovely colonial bungalow we'd just decided to rent in a pleasant suburban street in Johannesburg. 'We really must get this painted nicely,' my wife had said, looking at the squalid little hutch where the servants would live. 'These people are just animals,' the landlord had retorted in his heavy Austrian accent, 'you'd be wasting your money.'

I remembered standing in the sweltering heat of a library in central Johannesburg while a thoughtful black American politician explained to the attentive crowd why the most painful sanctions were necessary against South Africa. He told us about his own child, whose legs were twisted by some childhood disease and who had to wear leg-irons which caused him a lot of pain. The politician told us with tears in his eyes how hard it had been for him to fasten the irons on his son's legs every morning, with the child begging him not to do it because it hurt so much; how he'd had to keep on saying, 'Unless I do this, you'll never grow tall and straight,' and how each time his son had nodded and helped him to do up the buckles.

And now, here in Cape Town sixteen years later, we were giving thanks for the healing of the disease; achieved not through revolution and bloodshed but peacefully, by compromise, reconciliation and understanding. I suspect that I was much more conscious of the extraordinary changes that had come over this country than most of the congregation were. They, after all, had had four years to get used to the abandonment of apartheid and the move towards a pluralist society. To me the changes still seemed overwhelming. What they were celebrating was something rather different: the series of un-characteristic changes of heart which had brought us through the elections so peacefully. The series began with F.W. de Klerk, whom I'd known as a stony-faced minister of education. If you wanted a bigoted defence of apartheid, or someone to explain why Nelson Mandela had to stay in jail for the rest of his life, then F.W. de Klerk was your man. And he was the one who had let Nelson Mandela go.

Then, much later, came the other changes of heart: General Constand Viljoen broke away from the white irreconcilables and formed his Freedom Front party, which enabled even the far right to take part in the elections. And, even more importantly, Chief Man-gosuthu Buthelezi decided to give up his alarming campaign against the holding of the election (as a result of which hundreds of people had been killed and wounded) and to enter the lists with the other political parties. If you add to this the collapse of the white extremists, Eugene Terreblanche and the rest, and the failure of the brief terrorist campaign, then you can see that South Africa has a great deal to give thanks for at the moment. Of course things aren't always going to go this smoothly; the fierce accusations of ballot-rigging and the postponement of the formal announcement of Mandela's presidency show that. Countries don't live happily ever after, any more than people do. But the manner of a revolution dictates the pattern of the political system that follows it. A peaceful transfer of power is a pretty good assurance that however great the ensuing problems are, they won't be resolved violently.

On the evening of the day the thanksgiving service was held in Cape Town, I drove with my television crew to the beach to watch the sunset. As soon as we got there I recognized it: it was the beach on which I'd spent Christmas Day in 1977. They'd knocked down the low wall where the disconsolate black children had once sat, and in the last light of the setting sun a young coloured couple were drawing hearts in the sand and laughing when the waves washed them out. A little dog danced on the wet shore as the dark rich reds of the sky faded and the waters of the Atlantic went from amethyst to black. I've been fortunate to see many of the extraordinary changes that have come over our world, from the collapse of the Berlin Wall onwards. But I haven't seen anything better or more encouraging than what's been happening here.

AN UNRELENTING NIGHTMARE

ANDY KERSHAW   KIGALI   28 MAY 1994

The United Nations secretary-general was blaming the world com-
munity for allowing the slaughter to continue in Rwanda, and
there were suggestions that an early rebel victory would be the
most effective way of stopping the killing.

Lieutenant Henry N'Sengiyumva blinked over the bridge into the
River Nyabarongo, its swirling waters the colour of stewed tea. 'The
killing is slowing down,' he muttered. 'A week ago we were getting
nine hundred bodies a day in the river. Now it's down to about three
hundred.' As he spoke, the rigid corpse of a boy of about eight, still
wearing blue soccer-shorts, twirled by – his mouth wide open. A
woman was next, floating face-down in a floral dress. Her hands were
tied behind her back, her pants pulled down around her thighs.
'Sometimes they're shot or hacked to death first,' said the lieutenant,
'but often they just tie their hands and throw them in alive.'

'They' are the Rwandan government forces and their drunken
militias, the Interahamwe ('those who fight together') who have club-
bed, shot and macheted so many Rwandans that the bodies are beginning to pollute the gigantic Lake Victoria. Meanwhile, aid agencies
on the fringes of the butchery revise their estimated death toll steadily
upward towards a million.

In the ten minutes I spent with the Rwandan Patriotic Front (RPF)
unit guarding the bridge in this recently captured territory, just ten
kilometres south of the capital Kigali, nine swollen and stinking
corpses passed underneath us. What was, until early April, the second
most densely populated country on earth is now abandoned and
empty. Even the cows and goats, wandering about the deserted

villages, seem to be in a state of shock as they pick their way around the sad belongings dropped on the dirt road by terrified families. Those who ran fast enough are now sitting in muddy fields in neighbouring Burundi, Zaire and Tanzania.

I found some of those who did not make it in the village of Mayange, a cluster of mud-brick houses and a ransacked bar, silent but for birdsong and the drone of flies. Fifteen feet down, at the bottom of the village well, I saw and smelt a bloated human mush, six swollen heads and a tangle of limbs bristling with thousands of giddy bluebottles. And these were just the bodies on the surface. The RPF's priority is to stop the slaughter that the UN ran away from. The final push for Kigali, they say, will come when the army and its militias have been squashed in their stronghold in the west. They are fighting, they insist, not a tribal war but a campaign on behalf of all Rwandans – Tutsi and Hutu – to overthrow a genocidal and illegitimate government. Although predominantly Tutsi, there are many Hutus in the rebel ranks – three of my seven RPF guards were Hutu. And to feeding-stations and makeshift hospitals in RPF safe areas, like the town of Nyamata, the guerrillas bring refugees of both tribes. In the absence of aid agencies the mutilated are treated by RPF doctors. In Nyamata, I watched one RPF medic examine a young woman with an appalling head-wound. The crown had been sliced off, like the top of a pineapple, by an Interahamwe machete. She was, unbelievably, sitting there smiling at me and I could see her brain.

Things were going well for the RPF until last week. Its troops, well-disciplined and motivated, had secured most of the country. In RPF territory in the east refugees were beginning to return to work in their fields. Ordinary Rwandans are not relying on the return of the UN: the RPF is their security. But the RPF has got its own security problem. In areas long since liberated Interahamwe infiltrators, posing as RPF fighters, are bogging down, by ambush, the rebel advance. And they have recently got their hands on land-mines.

I know this because I walked over one last Tuesday. From the Nyabarongo bridge we drove our jeep a couple of miles down the dirt road towards Kigali. The track along the rim of a valley brought us up behind an RPF convoy of three trucks. It had stopped; I got out and walked up to the vehicle at the front to find out what was going on. To my horror, I found the truck on its side and the crater of a land-mine in the road. One guerrilla was slightly injured. I scampered back to the jeep to await the commander's instructions.

Absurd though it seems now, I carried on with a bit of work to take my mind off the danger so I was only half aware of the truck, twenty yards in front of us, when it started to reverse. Then there was a tremendous bang, a yellow flash and the truck flipped over like a beer-mat. I felt the heat of the blast on my face. Wreckage and rocks poured down. A crater had opened where I had just crossed the road. From the banana plantation across the valley came the echoes of spiteful laughter, jeering and howls of 'We are the Interahamwe!'

Then came the shooting. I heard the bullets fizzing through the roadside vegetation a spilt second before the sound of the gunfire crossed the valley. It was a textbook ambush. I flung myself into the ditch. It is astonishing how rational and calculating we were under fire. At this previously unpenetrated level of fear, a curious composure came over us. For ten minutes or so in the ditch we worked out our chances. It was an awful choice: we could escape by retracing our steps, but the Interahamwe were, said the RPF lads, advancing behind us. Our other option was to carry on down a road that was, clearly, full of mines to an RPF base six miles away. Taking the jeep was out of the question, as the weight would surely trigger more explosions. So we left a £16,000 Mitsubishi on a remote Rwandan hillside and set off, on foot with full kit, across the sights of death-squad snipers and prayed there were no anti-personnel mines. There were. I saw two in the first fifty yards. I knew that our chances of getting through were slender, and it was getting dark. We passed through a couple of empty villages. I could smell the corpses in the darkened, shattered houses from 200 yards away. As we tiptoed into the towns our RPF guards clicked off their safety catches. From the north we heard the boom of the big guns around Kigali. Every step towards safety was hell. Every one, I knew, might be my last. I walked, and waited for the bang.

Although I still feel drunk with the terror of that march, my own experience was trivial compared to the unrelenting nightmare thousands of Rwandans are living through every day. This afternoon, in government territory, hundreds more villagers will be pulled out of detention centres at random and butchered. Children are being hacked to pieces right now, and the world dithers. Every civilian I met in the country, mainly Tutsi but not all, said a total RPF victory was Rwanda's only hope. Only they, it's said, are capable of stopping the slaughter. But as long as the RPF's progress towards the killing fields is delayed by land-mines, Interahamwe ambushes or UN intervention, the increasingly desperate government killers may rush to complete their final solution for Rwanda. And Lieutenant N'Sengiyumva, on his grim vigil by the Nyabarongo river, will soon, I fear, lose count of the corpses altogether.

FOREST BURIAL

JEREMY BOWEN   DDIMO   9 JUNE 1994

The slaughter in Rwanda led to an exodus of refugees. They travelled in their hundreds of thousands to Burundi, to Tanzania, to Zaire and to Uganda, posing enormous logistical problems for the authorities there.

It was chilly in the forest. Our guide, a strong and earnest man called Fred Luzze, pulled on his jacket when we got out of the Land-Rover. Together we walked into the clearing where he had been directing operations for the past month. Fred is in charge of the men who collect and bury the bodies that are washed ashore on one small stretch of Lake Victoria's coastline, at Ddimo, a miserably poor Ugandan fishing village. About a dozen mounds of earth dominated the clearing. Fred explained that they were mass graves. He pointed over to an open pit: 'We will be needing another this afternoon,' he said. 'This one is almost full.' Mercifully, most of the corpses were already covered by a thin layer of soil, but the body of a child, of perhaps five or six years of age, was quite visible. Next to it were what I at first thought were rotten pieces of vegatation, things that might have just fallen in. They were, in fact, tangled human limbs, in an advanced state of decomposition.

As his men brought in more bodies, Fred Luzze talked about how hard he had tried to work out how human beings could slaughter their own kind with such brutality. He did not have an explanation, of course. He was just bowed down by what he had seen. He said that most of the bodies that the lake's currents had brought into Ddimo had been those of women and children. There had been boys and girls in school uniform, and babies, still wrapped in shawls and tied to the backs of their dead mothers. Some children, Fred told me, had been impaled on sticks, in threes and fours. Almost all of them had machete wounds. Not so many bodies are coming into Lake Victoria now. The genocidal killing in Rwanda has slackened off, at least for the time being. The Ugandan authorities have put a net across the mouth of the Kigara river, which flows out of Rwanda and into the lake. But rotting corpses, almost unrecognizable after weeks in the water, are still being washed up at places like Ddimo, and Fred and his men are still filling the mass graves in the clearing in the forest.

It was a relief to travel to Tanzania, to see Rwandans who had escaped the slaughter. Hundreds of thousands of them are still trying to leave the country, and two or three thousand arrive every day at the Benaco camp at Ngara. More than a quarter of a million people are already there. Not only is it the world's biggest refugee settlement, it has also become Tanzania's second biggest city. In British terms, it is as if a refugee population big enough to occupy Liverpool had arrived in the space of a single month. The local authorities are bemused, powerless to do anything to help the refugees. Usually, not very much happens in these parts. The district commissioner invited us to dinner to explain his problems. To get to his bungalow, we drove through an area of rolling, lush hills which looked like the Scottish borders. His residence was sheltered by rose bushes and rhododendrons, and inside he still hadn't taken down the Christmas decorations. A painting of the stable at Bethlehem hung over the fireplace. Dusty Christmas cards were displayed on strings, and the ceiling was hung with festive chains made of the polystyrene chips that usually come in packing cases.

The DC ordered a young district officer to pump up the pressure in the kerosene lamp. It hissed and sometimes it roared, and by its light he explained how the refugees at Benaco had put an intolerable burden on his province. It was, after all, about the most deprived corner of the world's second-poorest country. In days, the refugees had eaten all the area's reserves of food. Hundreds of them had descended on maize-fields and taken the half-grown crops. They were stripping the hillsides around the camp of trees, and this would ruin the land. He could not even survey the damage, because he did not have enough petrol for his car. Fortunately, the international relief agencies are working wonders at Benaco camp. It is a huge, sprawling place, but it is well organized, there is just enough to eat and there is clean water to drink. Best of all, nobody there is killing anybody else. That they might start, though, is the biggest fear of the agencies who run the camp. Without a shadow of doubt men and women who

were deeply involved in the killing are hiding there. So far, nobody
has tried to settle any scores.

The relief workers at Benaco Camp have other worries. They think
they could be swamped by another huge wave of refugees. They are
preparing contingency plans for 300,000. Inside Rwanda, it is much
too late to leave, for far too many people. Survivors of the killing, all
too often, are too traumatized to do much more than sit and wait for
it to happen to them. Sometimes they are so badly hurt that they
need special treatment, which is just not available. On an iron bed in
a schoolroom that had been turned into a ward lay a patient who was
so small I thought she was a child. I asked the nurses who she was,
but they did not know. She could not tell them, because she could
not speak. When they pulled back her blanket, I saw that a blow from
a machete had sliced across her face from ear to ear. There was a
deep gash where her mouth had been and most of her jaw was gone.
She gestured in my direction. I realized that she wanted my pen and
notebook. When I passed them over, she wrote that her name was
Emilien and that she was twenty-one. She wouldn't write down who
attacked her – she was too scared. Emilien pulled the blanket back
over her head, and I went away.

HELL ON EARTH

ROGER HEARING   GOMA   28 JULY 1994

Goma was once just a little-known town in Zaire, close to the border with Rwanda. But the arrival there of hordes of refugees from the Rwandan civil war led to one of Africa's greatest disasters. Goma became synonomous with tragedy and suffering on a biblical scale.

Two men came into Goma airport to die last week. They staggered to a grass verge, sectioned off by barbed wire from the journalists' tent, and lay down gasping. On the other side of the wire those who were keeping the world informed about the plight of more than a million refugees broke off from satellite telephone conversations to attempt to help. One man was already dead and the other one was taken off to hospital in an aid agency car. On one side of that barbed wire we were drinking water and eating French army field rations; on the other side, people were dying in their thousands from exhaustion, hunger and dehydration.

It is really only in disasters on this scale that the divisions among humans become so cruelly obvious. The haves and the have-nots: those condemned to a lingering death and those with the good fortune to be mere observers are separated by only a few inches of wire. It is not that most journalists can remain uninvolved observers in conditions like these, but it is generally futile and mostly counter-productive to attempt to help aid workers who actually know what they are doing. So we are left trying to take comfort from the indirect benefit we bring by trying to stir consciences and open chequebooks in the outside world. Any such benefit will probably be far too late for Andrew, a car mechanic I met as he walked vaguely past one of the bigger camps on the outskirts of Goma. He was one of the unfortunate, even amongst the blighted refugees of Rwanda. Born in

Uganda and seen still as an outsider, he was not put on any food aid lists and so was left to starve in the camp. He did not want to be there anyway; he had only fled with the others because he would have been labelled as an enemy spy and hacked to death with a machete if he had not. His mattress, with a few dollars sewn inside, the last of his payment from working on a feature film about Rwanda's mountain gorillas, was stolen at the border by Zairean soldiers, so now he had nothing. And, since there was little else he could usefully do, he had determined to keep on walking. He did not expect to survive the night, and I do not suppose he did. He is probably now one of the many thousand corpses thrown into the giant pits dug by the side of the airport road, his body distinguishable only by the fact that he had no one to wrap him in a rush mat, the modicum of dignity in death even the poorest of Rwandans is afforded by his relatives.

I wanted to help Andrew, but with the increasingly volatile crowd around him it would have started a riot. At least that is what I told myself, and by then he had melted back into the throng. I will remember his sad and dignified face for a long time. There is really no comfort here, and there are no lessons to be learned. If more than a million people leave their homes and flee into another country, even with the best planning in the world no aid agency can swing neatly into action, no health programme can stop the spread of diseases like cholera. Many aid workers feel acute frustration at their apparent impotence in the face of such suffering. That, plus the scenes of horror that resemble some allegorical medieval wall-painting, may have produced the idea that, in some awful way, these people have brought all this on themselves.

It was primarily members of the Hutu ethnic group who committed the appalling massacres at the beginning of the war in which perhaps a million, mainly Tutsis, died. There is strong evidence that the murderers and their supporters are now here, in Zaire, in the camps and dying with the rest of cholera and dehydration. I have heard normally rational and compassionate aid workers talk seriously about divine retribution. Apocalyptic scenes, perhaps, producing apocalyptic reasoning. But you only have to go into the camps to see that the innocent are suffering too: the children, the old, even the unborn and, as a collective punishment, this is harsh in the extreme.

I will remember the teacher, distraught to the point of hysteria because he had done all the doctors had told him, provided clean water and sugar solution drinks, and still his son was dying, stretched out on the jagged lumps of volcanic rock this land provides instead of soil. I suppose that, if a vengeful God were looking for a hell-like place to send these people, the lava fields outside Goma would fit the bill – right down to the choking black dust that blows all day into noses, eyes and throats and the active, glowering volcano that glows menacingly at night.

It is a measure of the unholy terror that has been let loose in Rwanda over the last four months that the green hills of their home, rich now with ripe fruit and corn and only a day's walk away, have enticed no more than three in a hundred of these refugees to go back. The fact that the rest are so terrified of reprisals by the new government is an indication that they do have blood on their hands, according to some. I think it is more to do with the nation needing some time to calm down after its collective nightmare, not wanting to take any risks until it is absolutely sure of itself, finding even a dreadful, but known, present better than an unknowable future.

It is easy to speculate from this side of the barbed wire. But trying to read the faces, to scrutinize the agony on the other side, to know the feelings of those children at the orphanage who, almost calmly, acknowledge that they are the last surviving member of their families, is certainly beyond me. I just hope that, deep inside, the horror of Goma is not being stored away to provide the fuel for the next conflagration, the power behind the machete that cuts into another Rwandan throat.

WESTERN AND EASTERN EUROPE

A MODEL EUROPE

SIMON CALDER   BILLUND   7 AUGUST 1993

As politicians throughout Europe argue about closer ties between the EU member states and whether or not they should adopt a common currency, there is one town in Europe that offers a vision of happy multinational coexistence. It's the Danish theme park of Legoland, built entirely from the plastic building blocks beloved by generations of children.

It is the ultimate plastic tourist attraction. Forty-two million small bits of Lego go to make up a theme park plonked in the middle of Denmark. The theme is conformity: if you are looking for heart-stopping thrills, don't go to Legoland. But it does boast its own hotel, its own restaurant and even its own airport. You can fly there direct from Britain every day of the week. You feel as though you are landing in a movie set in the near future, one of those films where humankind has evolved into a spookily ordered society. The sense of unreality starts when you step off the plane at Billund Airport, a massive terminal many miles from the nearest city. The trickle of passengers is easily outnumbered by the army of cleaners, clearing invisible specks of dust from already spotless tables. If this is the Europe of the future, it is worryingly sanitized.

So, where's Legoland? A cheerfully under-employed woman on the information desk pointed through the door: 'Behind the garage,' she said, 'about five minutes' walk.' That is a strange ethnocentric presumption, too. Why should I, a foreign visitor, be able arrogantly to assume that I can ask a local a question in English, and expect an immediate, and polite, response? Anyway, the park was only three minutes' walk away. You cannot pay to get in with Bank of Toytown money, but the equivalent of £10, payable in Danish kroner, Deutschmarks, ecus or even sterling, buys you an instant tour of the planet.

You can pan for plastic gold in Legorado, take a flight in a Legocopter, and learn more than you ever wanted to know about the story of Lego.

It is the story of standardization, of chipping away at individual faults and foibles. From making wooden toys between the wars, the company developed into a manufacturer of rigorously rectangular blocks, guaranteed to fit neatly together. If you ever wondered what happened to the odd brick that dropped down the back of the sofa in the mid-1970s, it – or 42 million others just like it – may have wound up here. The ultimate aim seems to be to recreate the world with millions of bits of plastic, orderly and controllable. The plastic planes at the building-block airport shuttle back and forth, encountering no air traffic control delays. The Taj Mahal coexists peacefully with the Acropolis, both of them protected by plastic miniatures of the White House and the Statue of Liberty.

Back in the real world, of course, attempts to make Europe fit more closely together are meeting with little success. The exchange rate mechanism, designed to bundle the currencies of Europe tightly together, has begun to unravel. The Maastricht Treaty has been ratified by Britain, but, like the Danes, the British insist on individual opt-out clauses. The avowed intent of the treaty is 'ever closer union', whose initial letters spell 'ecu'. But the single European currency is disdained by both Britain and Denmark, and they have negotiated escape routes on the track towards unity.

Something else links Britain and Denmark. The local newspaper, the *Legoland Times*, explains that the park is celebrating its silver jubilee. The company's next venture is to establish a Legoland in Britain, at Windsor, in three years' time. So what is in store for us? If a nation's tourist attractions are a reflection of itself, then Legoland speaks of orderliness bordering on obsession. Anyone who has met Danish people will know how inaccurate this image is, but if all you saw of Denmark was the area around Legoland you could be forgiven for concluding that this national stereotype is spot-on. Close to Legoland is the factory where the stuff is made. I peered in through a few windows. Every office seeks to outdo its neighbour in the scale and expertise of fanciful Lego creations: a menagerie of animals, a locomotive, a lunar landing vehicle. I wonder what they give each other for Christmas.

I wanted to see something of Denmark beyond the confines of building blocks, so I strolled into town, only to discover that Billund appears to be constructed entirely out of concrete cubes that look like giant prototypes for Lego bricks. I was back in the science fiction film, where the individual struggles against the stifling collective will. On the face of it, Legoland has little to offer any traveller who cherishes independence and discovering the unusual. But it is actually tremendous fun, especially the hands-on part. You can delve into the biggest toybox in the world, and indulge your wildest Lego fantasies. There is no age limit – anyone can borrow a boxful of bricks to build a meticulously planned creation, although youth is definitely an advantage. An eight-year-old took pity on my losing battle to build Colin the Crawling Caterpillar. He corrected my spatial ineptitude, and showed me how much Lego has advanced, with motors that work and wheels that are blissfully free of carpet fluff.

I also found out the secret of Legoland's wonderful plastic representations of the world's great structures. They do not just perch there, sturdy triumphs of the neat Lego system: they are glued together. I always regarded that as cheating, and I hope the company realizes that it will not be able to rearrange them should the world change – as I could do with Colin, the mechanical caterpillar who is now, miraculously, crawling.

TEETHING TROUBLES

MERIEL BEATTIE   BUDAPEST   26 AUGUST 1993

The main topic of conversation in Hungary concerns the country's prospects of joining the European Union. But do Hungarians have a realistic view of what Europe might be able to do for them?

It seems to be a favourite trick with dentists, perhaps to stop you thinking about the pain. Bent over, and with a needle poised above your gums, they suddenly throw in a question which is too complex just to be waved away or answered with a grunt. And that's what Dr Laszlo did: 'What do you think,' he said, lowering a metal prong towards my teeth, 'will Hungary succeed in getting into Europe?' There's not much anyone could have said right at that moment. But even after the drilling, the scraping, the rinsing and the swilling were over, Dr Laszlo, his partner in his busy private dental surgery and their young technician seemed genuinely keen to hear whatever answer I could mumble out beneath the local anaesthetic. And they're not the only ones.

For a large number of Hungarians, this question seems to be something of an obsession. In many cities your taxi-driver, the man on the bus or the car mechanic might want to know what you, as a foreigner, think their football team's chances might be for the World Cup qualifiers. Or they might ask whether or not you think they'll get to host the next Olympic Games. In Hungary they are more likely to ask you about their chances of getting promoted to what is seen as the most important premier division side of all, Europe. It's hard to answer this question, not just when there's a dentist chipping away inside your mouth, but because different groups of Hungarians have different ideas of what Europe actually means and what is to be done to get there. Politicians, as you'd expect, talk about specific targets, encouraging foreign trade to revitalize the economy and

48

joining structures like the European Union. Beyond this, the prime minister, Joszef Antall, holds the idea of belonging to Europe aloft as a kind of Holy Grail – getting to it is a quest through which Hungary will cleanse itself of the dark stains of communism. He rarely wastes an opportunity to tell any audience, be it parliament or a gathering of boy scouts, that Europe is the only way ahead.

Ambitious professionals have a slightly different view. For them, Europe is where you can, at long last, get a just financial reward for your professional skills. But it's not just a question of grabbing a fast buck or Deutschmark. Getting to Europe is like entering a select club: aspiring members have to prove themselves, and the way you do that is to invest all your time and capital in providing a service that will outstrip competitors. Take Dr Laszlo. I had to find a dentist – fast – when the crowns on my front teeth shattered in a particularly crusty Hungarian bread roll. Not having the time to drive to my last dentist in Vienna, I turned in desperation to the classified advertisements in Budapest's English-language weeklies. Astonishingly there were five or six dentists, four private health clinics and even three plastic surgeons. I picked Dr Laszlo's Dental Express, the one that advertised 'Austrian quality at Hungarian prices'.

Despite the slogan, I'd steeled myself for some primitive carpentry and quite possibly the added expense of a later trip to Vienna for repairs. But there was nothing primitive about the hi-tech surgery, complete with tropical fish and glossy business magazines, that I walked into. Whirling between patients on his stool-on-wheels, Dr Laszlo performed, between questions, a superb repair job. He and his team work from 8 a.m. until late at night if necessary, and they seem obsessed with customer satisfaction. Worried that the new porcelain crowns they'd created in what struck me as record time might not quite match, they made three trips with me out into the garden to check in natural light. They needn't have worried. They were a perfect fit, and cost a fraction of the price I would have paid in Austria.

All this probably sounds very positive – indeed it is if, as I did, you need a specialist urgently and have the money to pay for the treatment. But there are a couple of worrying aspects to Hungary's race for what it sees as Europe. One is the feeling that it's a question of one-upmanship; not just keeping abreast of the Czechs and Slovaks and other would-be EU members, but actually beating them to it. Whoever gets there first will be a sort of king of the castle, in a better position to get what it wants from whoever is still crossing the draw-bridge. Two months ago, when Slovakia was getting ready to be accepted as a member of the Council of Europe, Hungary, which is already a member, threatened to block its accession over a bilateral squabble about minorities. In the end Hungary backed down, but the incident looked pretty much like a dress rehearsal for what will happen when the central European countries get into the EU.

Another disturbing aspect is the feeling that some people are getting so obsessed by the idea of getting to Europe as quickly as possible that social problems at home are not getting the attention they need. When, in answer to the inevitable question, I told the furniture removal man that I thought Hungary's chances were very good, he frowned and shook his head. 'But we've so many poor people here,' he said, 'so many Trabants still on the road.' For him, those people who didn't have businesses, or the flashy cars that go with them, spoiled Hungary's image. Marketeers have not been slow in catching on to this. Many advertisements for businesses and products feature a smug little EU flag at the bottom – if it says Europe on the packet, it must be better. A classic example is a famous brand of washing powder, which in Britain used to claim to 'wash whiter than white'. In Hungary it promises to clean your clothes to 'peak European quality'.

There's little doubt that Hungary will one day become a member of the European Union. It must be hoped that Hungarians will, by then, have a more realistic idea of what it can do for them.

SUFFER THE CHILDREN

BILL HAMILTON   BERAT   16 SEPTEMBER 1993

Two years after the broadcast of his harrowing television and radio reports on the treatment of Albania's disabled children, Bill Hamilton returned to the country to see how money raised by Western charities was being spent. He found that conditions had improved at some homes and hospitals ... but that at others they were worse than ever.

Their necks craned through the distorted iron bars, children – some as young as three, and dressed only in a few ill-fitting rags – watched our arrival in almost total disbelief. I had come with BBC cameraman Bhasker Solanki to view the place a confidant had described as the nearest thing to hell on earth – a children's home in the Albanian resort of Berat, in which the country's former Stalinist dictator had decreed the city's mentally ill and physically disabled children should be locked out of sight and out of mind. Visitors had come here before, but despite promises of help few had returned.

The building was nothing more than a decaying shell – no glass in the windows, no electric light, no heating. The nurse ushered us along the dark, forbidding corridor. Her hand stretched out to head height to pull the latch that kept most of the children imprisoned in a foul-smelling, stone-floored room furnished only with an old wooden bench that looked likely to fall apart at any moment.

The conditions were akin to those of the Middle Ages. One girl, her naked body covered in flies and sores, hid her face from sight. A little boy scoured the filthy floor looking for scraps to eat. Another, just seven years old, desperate to quench his thirst, was lapping water from the top of a bath like an animal at a trough. Others, clearly sedated, seemed frozen to the spot – ghostly figures deprived of even the merest touch of human dignity.

Upstairs, the situation was little better. Children with wasted limbs lay motionless in their rusted cots or were spreadeagled across the floor. Dritan, aged just four, was tied to the bars of his cot – to prevent him from injuring himself, said the nurses. How, I wondered, was it possible for such horrors to be visited upon the innocent and most vulnerable, even in Europe's most impoverished country? I had witnessed similar scenes two years before in the northern city of Shkoder. Thankfully, aid and expertise from Britain, France and Italy have transformed life for the children there who had been starved of love, proper attention and any form of stimulation.

The government in Tirana was not slow in expressing its shame over what we had witnessed. The problem is that, faced with seemingly insuperable odds, Albania can spend only $10 on each of its 3.2 million citizens in the current financial year. When salaries and desperately needed hospital reconstruction are taken into account, to say nothing of purchasing even the most basic medicines, then there is precious little left with which to treat the sick and dying.

Fortunately, the world is heeding Albania's cry for help, even though the war in nearby Bosnia has blunted the effectiveness of the response. So desperate is the country for foreign aid and investment that its democratic president, Sali Berisha, is playing a three-card trick with pleas to Brussels, Washington and Jeddah all at the same time. He has been trying to improve links with the European Community, he has pleaded his case with the Americans, and he has also signed Albania up as a member of the Islamic Conference. Kuwait, in particular, has responded by investing substantial sums into a development fund to reconstruct hospitals and mosques and breathe life back into the main port, Durres. There's even a place for the country's old communist ally, China, in the investment stakes as the new government tries to get the economy moving.

Inflation, which was running at 300 per cent just a year ago, has now been brought under control, with the price of some essential food items such as cooking oil and flour actually falling. This has been achieved by a combination of tight budgetary control, international food aid and a duty imposed on all imported products in order to stimulate domestic food production.

But the continuing international sanctions on Albania's neighbour, Montenegro, have badly hit the economy. At least sixty private firms have gone bankrupt and Albania's only international rail link with the former Yugoslavia has been shut down. The country's infrastructure, vital for attracting foreign investment, is in a woeful state. The government is targeting the World Bank for long-term loans for the reconstruction of essential services such as roads, transport and telecommunications. Only one per cent of Albanians have a telephone, and a new digital exchange donated by the Norwegian government lies idle because there are no cables to connect it to the rest of the system.

In Europe's poorest country, the problems are so overwhelming that without continuing and substantial outside help, Albania simply cannot cope. This is why the children of Berat, distressed incomprehension in their eyes, reach out fragile arms to strangers like me, desperate for food and affection.

C'EST UNE VIE DE CHIEN

STEPHEN JESSEL   PARIS   18 SEPTEMBER 1993

Life for the BBC's Paris Correspondent underwent a considerable change with the arrival of a new addition to his family.

We knew when we brought him home for the first time that January afternoon that life could never be quite the same again. The days would have to start earlier, bedtimes would be later, social life would inevitably be affected. There were other considerations too: the French are famously tolerant in such cases, but would it be possible to take him out to cafés and restaurants? What about travelling, staying in hotels, preparing his food? Suppose it was necessary to go away at short notice? Getting a dog certainly complicates your existence. The circumstances under which the animal bounded into our life are too shaming to go into. After half a century of principled and active opposition to dogs – not least because of their somewhat casual approach to personal hygiene – a deadly combination of an only child and sustained moral blackmail wore me down. Of the creature himself, the less said the better. He came from the equivalent of the Battersea Dogs' Home, where they were desperate to be rid of him for reasons instantly obvious to anyone setting eyes on him. His parentage can only be a matter of the most fantastic conjecture; I overheard at the Bois de Vincennes a mother say to a child: 'No, chéri, it isn't a monkey.'

Each day he has to be taken long distances across Paris to be exercised, and not, you may be sure, by the moral blackmailer whose pet he is supposed to be. Fortunately our flat has a long corridor along which he can hurtle, in the course of a singularly witless game involving a pair of old socks. To anyone contemplating buying a dog in Paris, I would counsel deep thought lasting, say, half a second, followed by an unshakeable decision never to do so.

It would be much wiser to take up a simpler, less expensive pastime such as running a Formula One racing-car team or collecting Rembrandts. In France it costs between three and four times as much to go to the vet as it does to visit the doctor. The kennels where he stays from time to time provide rooms with cable television, mini-bars and a chocolate laid on the pillow each night – at least I assume from the price that they do. Anybody can acquire a dog. It takes a real fool to adopt a lame animal, but that is what has happened.

Our four-legged friend is more of a three and three-quarter-legged friend, his front right paw being deformed either from birth or by an accident. The estimated cost of the operation to put this right is more than my entire gross annual salary when I started earning a living in the mid-1960s. And yet this animal has provided a useful insight into life in Paris. The British may regard themselves as sentimental about animals, but they should look across the Channel. There are ten million dogs in France, more than the number of children aged under twelve. Paris alone is home to between two hundred thousand and a quarter of a million, requiring the attentions of squads of green-overalled motorcyclists with special vacuum cleaners to restore pavements to an acceptable state.

The French can be cruel to their animals, as can some other nations. I am haunted by the sad eyes of an old Labrador abandoned in the Bois de Boulogne, tied to a tree, unable to comprehend so cynical a betrayal. But in general the reverse is true. Pets are doted on, and this is what getting a dog has disclosed. All the rules are suspended, including social ones. Parisians never talk to strangers, except in the presence of a dog when long chats about pedigree – not a very long chat in our case – or about health, temperament and age are freely permitted. As for the law, it is simply ignored. In one of the cheese shops in the local market the first thing the eye sees is a notice stating that by decree of the local authority animals are not allowed to enter. The second thing one sees is the owner's Yorkshire terrier seated at the cash desk.

There are regulations governing animals on public transport. Apart from guide dogs, they are tolerated only if small and carried in some kind of container or bag. No one takes much notice, especially on the metro. Backed by an enchanting series of Ronald Searle cartoons and fines of up to £150, a campaign against the fouling of streets was launched a couple of years ago, but there have been only a handful of summonses and fines. Earlier fears about problems with hotels and restaurants were quite unfounded. Indeed, the red Michelin guide actually has a symbol for those establishments which won't let animals in, the assumption being that in the normal course of events they will. André, who runs the bistro round the corner from the cheese shop, also has a Yorkshire terrier, a giant photo of which decorates the bar, and went to Italy for his holidays this year. He returned outraged. They wouldn't let his pet into the public rooms of hotels or onto the beach.

When I tell people about the quarantine regulations in Britain, where dogs don't have to be vaccinated and identifiable through a tattoo in the ear as is the case in France, they refuse to believe me. To get to know the people in the *quartier*, get a pet. It'll reveal a dimension you didn't suspect. Off-hand waiters in cafés regularly nominated for European surliness awards will, unasked, bring bowls of water. And you realize, too, how many people in Paris are lonely. There may be something slightly absurd about the middle-aged businessman with his unsmiling face walking his primped and clipped poodle, but perhaps half the inhabitants of the capital live by themselves and for them *Toutou* may be much more than a toy. In a glittering but hard-hearted city, he may, quite literally, be a best friend.

MACHO ROMANIA

ANDY KERSHAW   BUCHAREST
7 OCTOBER 1993

The fall of the dictator Ceausescu has led to an upsurge in racial tension in Romania, with gypsies and ethnic Hungarians suffering most from Romanian machismo and boorishness.

The old woman was struggling to drag a handcart of potatoes out of the field and up the grass bank at the side of the road. We sprang down to give her a hand. 'You,' she said, jabbing a finger at my friend once the cart was rattling along the tarmac, 'you, gentleman! Romanian man, no gentleman.' I was relieved to hear this. After five days in macho Romania I was beginning to worry that I was some kind of an irredeemable wimp.

The crash course in boorishness began before clearing customs at Bucharest Airport. At the immigration desks – two of the sixteen were open – there was no queue, but a heaving human blockage. If the guy who almost shoved me off my feet had said 'excuse me' first I might have responded to the message on his companion's lapel badge: 'Operation Smile International'. Indifferent to the bedlam all about them, a couple of chain-smoking, dog-faced soldiers in greasy fatigues prodded a cleaning lady into sweeping up their fag ends from the empty diplomatic channel. Smoking is, I think, compulsory in Romania. After an hour or so, I hadn't moved an inch closer to the passport check. Other passengers were, quite unselfconsciously, pushing in at the front. If this is how post-communist individualism is flourishing in Romania and if the Romanian approach to the free market free-for-all is a similar scramble, everyone but the fattest, rudest and most thuggish will find themselves at the back of the queue. And behind them will be the gypsies.

Never before on my travels have I come across such universal and casual ethnic hatred. A grinning government translator pointed to a group of people on a Bucharest street. 'You see these? They are gypsies,' he said. 'I would like to do away with them altogether. They give a bad impression to tourists. Seriously, I would like to kill them.'

'You give a bad impression to tourists,' I snapped, a hair's breadth from smacking him in the mouth. Later, at a traffic light, the driver in front opened his door as the light turned green, hitting a gypsy child washing windscreens. Most frightening is to see this hatred in supposedly educated and sophisticated Romanians. They are astonished that anyone should imagine that their attitudes are offensive; gypsies are responsible for all the crime in their country, they will tell you. And although they have lived there for a thousand years, gypsies are not, it is argued, real Romanians.

'It's suicide to go in there,' said another guide when I told him we were going to the gypsy village of Clejani to find a group of internationally renowned musicians. A few hours later, sitting in the bandleader's garden enjoying robust gypsy hospitality – bread, cheese, olives, plum brandy and wild music, I leaned over the table to the guide. 'Suicide?' I asked. He said nothing but kept on eating. That, I thought, was the end of that. But the next day, as we were approached by two gypsy children selling postcards, he turned to me with undisguised contempt. 'Here come your friends,' he snarled.

Ethnic hatred is a price half of eastern Europe and God knows how much of the former Soviet Union is now paying for democracy. Yet no one I met in Romania could see the danger in an irrational loathing similar to that which has dehumanized neighbouring Yugoslavia. The forty-year communist denial of history had swept these ancient tensions under the carpet. Nicolae Ceausescu knew the threat and tried to compress into a single Romanian identity the ethnic Hungarian, gypsy and Jewish minorities and the majority, who call themselves, with no sense of irony, 'true Romanians'. But since the old monster was put up against the wall and shot at Tirgoviste barracks on Christmas Day 1989 following Europe's most violent revolution, older demons have been squirming out of hibernation in basements from Brasov to Bucharest.

I ran into a few of them in a former headquarters of the Securitate, Ceausescu's secret police. A hand-painted banner on the railings in front of this shelled and burned-out building invited us in to see the Museum of the Resistance. Obviously this would be an exhibition dedicated to the brave demonstrators who, in December 1989, stood unarmed before Securitate guns and army tanks just a couple of blocks down the street. In the cellar, whitewashed walls, halogen spot-lighting and pony-tailed youths in denim jackets gave a reassuring sense of the artistic and intellectual. It looked like any other art college degree show. But the music was wrong: lusty, Germanic military marches boomed from a ghetto-blaster. One of the organizers, Leonard, a soft-spoken lad of about twenty, showed me round. Here were copies of pre-war newspapers reporting the murder in prison in 1938 of Corneliu Zelea Codreanu, the founder of the Iron Guard – Romania's fascists. Below them were the writings of his successor, Horia Sima, who, supporters believed, carried the sword of an archangel. 'Are you a fascist?' I asked Leonard. 'I am a Christian and a nationalist,' he said.

A prim young woman, with the expressionless face of a Victorian doll, handed me a list of writers banned under the communists: Rudolf Hess, Joseph Goebbels, Adolf Hitler. It was chilling to find the fascists reinvented, in the ideological confusion of post-Ceausescu Romania, as symbols of freedom and resistance – and in a government building at that. Leonard and his friends in the basement may not make up a mass movement but the fascists' reappearance, amid conditions ideal for a retreat into nationalism and authoritarianism, is not promising. There is widespread resentment of President Ion Iliescu's National Salvation Front government. The heroes of Christmas 1989 are, say many Romanians, the same old career communists and Securitate generals who ran the place before. 'No, it was not a revolution,' said a bus driver who overheard me describing it thus. 'It was a Securitate revolution. Just change of leader. Not people's revolution.' There is much evidence to support the view that the military, Securitate and party chiefs orchestrated the uprising only to remove Ceausescu.

Few have benefited from the country flinging itself into the free market. Romanians are now noticing a vast fault-line between rich and poor. On the same street I saw a Ferrari Testarossa parked on the pavement and a horse-drawn cart, loaded with hay, coming the other way. Inevitably, economic tensions such as these will lead to further political turmoil. But scapegoats are at hand: more than a million gypsies and nearly two million ethnic Hungarians. They rehearsed a little ethnic cleansing in 1990 when a number of gypsy villages were burned by non-gypsy neighbours. In Transylvania attacks on Hungarians led to six deaths and three days of mob violence. It's an explosive mixture waiting for a spark – and for that, you need look no further than the violent machismo that you feel is always just below the surface of routine charmlessness. Arriving at a hotel in Suceava, and loaded down with a mighty rucksack, I was twice shoulder-charged out of the way – once by the manager. Outside the Hotel Bucharesti, as I waited for a taxi and listened to the music from a gypsy wedding reception across the street, an argument started between a wedding guest and a motorist parked at the kerb. The gypsy ran indoors and reappeared waving a length of steel piping. The driver reached into the glove-box and whipped out a pistol. For a couple of minutes everything went into slow motion. They pushed and shoved each other and I cowered behind the gunman's car, until hotel security men eventually persuaded them to calm down and come inside for a drink.

Drink had been taken too at my hotel in the mountains of Transylvania. Locals had told me that if I went out the back after dark, to where the kitchens emptied their rubbish, it was possible to see bears. They came down from the forest at night to rummage for a free meal. To my amazement, as I stood on a grassy hillock above the dump, there was the black bulk of an enormous bear gently rooting through the bins. When it stood up and turned to watch me, eyes flashing in the torchlight, it was a good six feet tall. The magic was too brief. From the hotel doorway three drunken youths scrambled up the bank, a sub-human swarm of boils and bum-fluff. Their laughter was unmistakably malicious. Spotting the great beast, and with no regard whatever for my interest in it, they reacted as though by reflex. From a flowerbed they snatched up rocks and stoned the bear.

Should the tensions within Romania ever tear the country apart, I reflected later in a rage at their mindless aggression, the young thugs might get what they deserve. I imagined them in a civil war foraging through dustbins to survive. And I pictured a huge and hungry bear swaggering out of the shadows and ripping them limb from limb.

PENSIONERS AND MOLOTOVS

KEVIN CONNOLLY   MOSCOW   9 OCTOBER 1993

The world looked on anxiously as hardline opponents of President Yeltsin launched a bid to take control of the country. Street-fighting erupted in the centre of Moscow, and tanks opened fire on the Russian parliament building.

Her face, when she lifted it from the crumpled Red Flag in which it had been buried, was twisted with rage and grief, her eyes bloodshot from weeping. Her husband stood dazed and shaking beside her, holding a piece of clean cloth that I had found in my pocket against a cut on the side of his head. Purple blood oozed through his trembling fingers. He was making his way towards an ambulance with the unmistakeable look of shock in his eyes, a look that reminds you of a child trying not to cry. His wife stopped him and held him by the shoulders until an American television crew was ready to film, and then she pushed him gently forward again, shouting into the microphone that Russia's communists and nationalists were being brutally repressed.

'Is your Yeltsin doing this for democracy?' she screamed at us as the camera turned and the ambulance drove off. We were left, half a dozen reporters and perhaps a hundred demonstrators, surrounded by long menacing rows of riot police, each with the careful, stony stare into the middle distance which is the hallmark of the men who do such things all over the world. If you could be ordered at any moment to baton-charge a crowd, I suppose the last thing you want is eye contact with anyone in it. The old lady turned to the huge statue of Lenin that dominates the lifeless square of white concrete government buildings and raised her hands like a supplicant.

'Protect us ...' she started to say, but her voice was lost in the roar of another police loudspeaker announcement warning the crowd to disperse. They began to drift off, and when we followed them a few moments later we left October Square lined with riot-police officers staring impassively through the curious mixture of tourists and shoppers who had watched the demonstration. It was only an hour before we picked up the demonstrators again, but this time the mood was very different. We had swung out onto the Moscow ring-road in front of the imposing Foreign Ministry building to find two troop-trucks bearing down on us along the wrong side of the road.

An American agency photographer striding ahead of them raised his eyebrows and patted his flak jacket. As we drove over the road and into a side street we got our first glimpse of the thousands of protesters now striding with real purpose around the ring-road to the beleaguered Russian parliament building, the White House. They looked like the crowds you see in Stalinist-era films about the Bolshevik revolution, moving quickly, in step and with an air of real menace.

One of Alexander Rutskoi's advisers was a few hundred metres ahead of them, half-walking, half-jogging backwards, trying to steady himself as he tried to take a photograph. He did not seem to manage it, but you could see why he wanted to. In the air above the crowd a huge banner of the extreme right-wing National Salvation Front billowed like a boiling cloud of silk. Around it a hail of bricks and bottles flew, steadily driving back the police lines. The air was alive with an animal sound that mingled fear, excitement and hostility; the sound of protesters nerving themselves to assault armed police, the sound, in truth, of a crowd turning into a mob.

The police finally stood their ground near the ring-road but they had left it too late. There was a bizarre, almost theatrical, quality to the brief stand-off that followed. A few cameramen took their last chance to film from the middle ground. We all have our views about the best vantage point from which to cover riots and shoot-outs, but no one thinks it is from between the two sides. The police began to fire tear-gas shells towards us, and above the rising muffled roar of the crowd you could hear the occasional flat boom of an officer's pistol. But even then the police were edging backwards and it was then, through the sour, choking clouds, that the crowd attacked.

Caught up in the moment, I found myself carried along by the first wave of protesters. They were moving so quickly as the police fled that they overran bus after bus filled with Interior Ministry reinforcements. Stripped of their discipline, helmets off inside buses surrounded by screaming protesters smashing windows with iron bars, they were simply overwhelmed. The aura of frightening authority on which they rely was gone. I saw one, face streaked with dirt, sobbing with fear as he handed his riot shield and helmet to one of the demonstrators' leaders. Beside him another officer, and it did occur to me in a banal sort of way how young he looked, was shaking so much that he could not unfasten the strap on his helmet to give it away.

Suddenly an old lady appeared, dragging a child – presumably her own grandchild – along in one hand and clutching a half-brick in the other. 'The streets are ours,' she was shrieking, 'the people have won.' We were now almost at the White House, and faces were appearing at the windows as the hardliners who had been holed up there for almost a fortnight came to see the people they believed had come to rescue them. Then, suddenly, there was the unmistakeable crackle of machine-gun fire as the authorities made one final effort to regain control of the streets. It is a curiously undramatic sound when you hear it so close, but when you listen to a tape-recording afterwards the note of fear in your own voice and the click of bullets striking the road surface restore all the drama you would care for, and a little more besides.

It was, of course, at that moment that the men inside the White House – hardly rational, you would think, after ten days and nights inside bolstering each other's drunken courage to fight to the last drop of blood – lost their grip on reality. They began to see themselves, even as the Red Army was rolling towards Moscow to crush their ragged revolt, as revolutionary heroes. In their own minds they were dispatching armies to seize power. In fact they were sending young men to die assaulting the well-armed, well-disciplined government forces who were not liable to panic and flee like the inexperienced young riot policemen.

There was much more to see, of course, and much more to be reported, like the ferocious gun-battle for the control of the television tower, where crowds of onlookers gathered and pensioners with Molotov cocktails urged everyone to join in the fight. The next day, when the tanks rolled onto the bridge over the White House, for a few uncertain moments we did not know whose side they were on. Then their barrels swivelled towards the White House, and Mr Yeltsin was safe. The first round they fired sent an echoing roar around the city centre, a symbolic message of brutal force to the White House defenders. It also – and you note these things almost subconsciously – stopped the clock on the front of the parliament building.

It was a tense and often terrifying weekend and yet bizarrely, however close I was to the gunfire, there always seemed to be at least one spectator – a man walking his dog, an old lady clutching a string bag of groceries – apparently oblivious to the historic and violent drama that stunned Moscow and shocked the world.

HISTORY REPEATS ITSELF

BRIDGET KENDALL MOSCOW
9 OCTOBER 1993

Following October's coup attempt, our correspondent looked to see whether parallels could be drawn with the bid, two years earlier, to oust Mr Yeltsin's predecessor, President Gorbachev.

Walk across the bridge that links the Ukraine Hotel to Novy Arbat, look across the river and you will see the favourite tourist view in Moscow: not Red Square and the gaudy squirls and domes of St Basil's Cathedral, but the half-blackened shell of what was called the White House – the relic of last week's rebellion. Before long an eager-faced man in a shabby coat will come up and ask if you want him to take a photo, instant polaroid evidence that you were there too, an eyewitness to Russia's second October revolution. In fact it was not really a revolution; it was more of a revolt, madcap and hopeless and led by a desperate band whose biggest mistake was to believe in their own delusions of grandeur and take literally their own clumsy and dangerous rhetoric. I was comforted to find, as I walked on over the bridge, that the crowds of Russian sightseers gathered in groups to discuss what it all meant seemed as uncertain and confused as I was. Usually street debates in Moscow turn into angry polemics, each side bent on browbeating its opponents. But this time no one seemed to have an answer. 'Well, what would you have done if you were president?' one man asked another in exasperation. 'We could not go on living in that anarchy.'

What is particularly confusing is the way events have repeated themselves, echoing the failed coup of August 1991, but all back to front and inside out, a sort of parody of recent history. For a start some of the players are the same: Boris Yeltsin, Ruslan Khasbulatov, Alexander Rutskoi, in 1991 the top three defenders of Russian democracy. The staging, too, is identical: White House versus the Kremlin. But this time Boris Yeltsin is in the Kremlin, and have not some of his actions been rather like those of the hardline coup leaders two years ago?

Just consider this: on 21 September the Russian president brazenly disregards the constitution and dissolves parliament in order to usurp power. When he is challenged he brings tanks onto the streets of Moscow to crush the resistance. As the population watches aghast, he declares a state of emergency in the capital, bans street-rallies, suspends opposition parties, imposes censorship on all but a few loyal newspapers, and, as a sop to the masses, orders new bread subsidies for the needy. Meanwhile, opposition leaders, once again holed up in the Russian parliament building, set about organizing resistance. They appeal to the people of Moscow to come and protect them. They urgently summon parliamentarians to sit in emergency session. They vote to oust the tyrant president and set up an alternative government. They call on the army and police to defect to their side. They appeal to the United Nations to back their cause. And just in case their citadel is stormed, they make plans for an alternative seat of government in the provinces.

No wonder Ruslan Khasbulatov and Alexander Rutskoi thought they were on a winning streak. Hadn't they been through all this two years ago when Boris Yeltsin was on their side, and didn't they come out victorious? Hadn't the whole world applauded when they saw the famous cellist Mstislav Rostopovich cradling a machine-gun as he kept guard in the White House? But this time, of course, it was different. Neither the West nor the people of Moscow rallied to the White House. The crowd outside the parliament never swelled to more than a few thousand. In other Russian cities demonstrations were even more pathetic: small crowds of just a few hundred. Inside the parliament, one by one the deputies crept away, to take advantage of a generous redundancy offer from President Yeltsin, leaving a hard core made up mainly of communist activists. And despite boasts from General Rutskoi and his defence and security ministers, there were no mass defections from the armed forces. Military leaders may have been reluctant to obey President Yeltsin's orders, but they were even more unwilling to sacrifice their neutrality for Mr Khasbulatov's diminishing parliament.

But the point really was that behind the pure white facade of the parliament building, the resistance to Boris Yeltsin had little to do with democracy. Those of us who listened to talk around the campfires outside the White House night after night know how racist, xenophobic and aggressive the mood was. The favourite subjects of conversation were whether Boris Yeltsin was a Jew, and whether he was working for the American CIA or an international Zionist conspiracy.

Mr Khasbulatov's Supreme Soviet had long since ceased to function as a respectable parliament. By the end neither he nor his hardline deputies had any regard for procedure. They ruthlessly used the parliament as a shield, first to organize nationwide sabotage of Mr Yeltsin's reforms, and then to gather arms and ammunition. And when last Sunday Mr Khasbulatov and Alexander Rutskoi called on their ragged, exuberant supporters to take over the television station and attack the Kremlin, they made a fatal mistake. Russians watching it all live on cable television were shocked and angry. Many had thought Alexander Rutskoi was a decent if misguided man; now he was openly inciting the crowd to violence.

The parallels with 1991 continue. Ironically, the lawyers who have come forward to defend the now-imprisoned rebels are the same lawyers who defended the August coup leaders. It really does feel as though history is repeating itself. One person who is determined it should not, however, is Boris Yeltsin himself. Two years ago, he disappeared on holiday for a month to take stock and, by his own admission, lost the initiative. This time round he is acting quickly. He has banned the communists again, but he has also got rid of the Constitutional Court, so there is no one to reinstate them. Now he is putting pressure on Russia's regions and republics to agree to disband their local parliaments and councils. The unspoken threat is that if they object, then what happened in Moscow could happen to them: emergency rule, troops, and an end to regional autonomy.

Will Yeltsin's gamble work, and will the regions cave in? Or will the parallels go further, and will they, like the Soviet republics two years ago, rush instead to declare independence from Moscow? However, the worst worry is that a pattern is setting in. As Russia painfully shakes off its communist past, lurching from crisis to crisis, will we start getting used to the news that there has been a new coup attempt in Moscow?

WINNERS AND LOSERS

ALLAN LITTLE FOČA 16 OCTOBER 1993

As talks aimed at ending the war in Bosnia started, re-started and dragged on, the 'ethnic cleansing' continued and it became clear that no one was going to stop a powerful army determined to use force to change border lines.

I had met so many of its former residents, mostly Muslims expelled during the first ferocious days of ethnic cleansing, that by the time I came to visit Foča it had already acquired in my imagination a precise and malign character. Foča: for me the very name has a ring to it. It conjures up images of forced expulsions, summary execution, the burning of homes and the kind of mass terror that, in a matter of days, uproots whole populations from land they and their ancestors have occupied for centuries.

It sits in a deep, steep-sided valley on the River Drina, the focal point of an expansive wooded hinterland. It was through these hills that, in April and May of last year, most of the people of Foča fled, many of them on foot, walking for days, not knowing in which direction safe territory lay. You cannot visit Foča without written permission from the government of a state no one in the world recognizes: the so-called 'Republika Srpska', that ethnically homogenous ministate whose foundation was the very purpose of the war. Ethnic cleansing was the agent of its creation. Ethnic cleanliness in future is the guarantee of its continued existence.

The deputy mayor of Foča, Ljubo Todović, was unapologetic. 'Of course the Muslims left, in all wars there are winners and losers,' he said with a shrug of his shoulders. There is no doubt about who has won this one and Foča, a town that until eighteen months ago had a Muslim majority, is one of the spoils. Todović showed us round his ethnically pure fiefdom with the relaxed self-confidence of a man

68

who knows that victory has been achieved and that there will be no turn of the tide. It is a miserable Mary Celeste of a town; every other house is empty or destroyed. The shops and bars are gutted and there is scarcely a sign, even eighteen months after the successful cleansing of the place, of any serious effort to rebuild. Timber was Foča's main industry, now it is the town's main supply of fuel; everywhere the streets are piled with logs, cut and neatly stacked outside every home and public building as the people prepare for another winter without the public utilities that almost everywhere else in Europe are taken for granted. We went into a bakery to buy bread. 'When are you people going to send us food?' the woman behind the counter said. 'We've nothing to eat here, there's just nothing.' The deputy mayor, at our heels throughout, told her to shut up. 'Nobody asked you to speak,' he said. 'Speak when you're spoken to.'

I know a man in Sarajevo from whom almost everything in life has been stolen in order to build Republika Srpska. His name is Suad. He's thirty-five, married with one son, and he is one of the 16,000 Muslims who were driven from Foča. A few days after the war began he took his family to Goražde. It was clear, he said, that Foča would fall and that it would be impossible for Muslims to stay there. He had intended to go back the next day to collect his parents, but by then there were Serbian army road-blocks and the town was inaccessible.

Suad had no home in Goražde, so he got on a bus with his wife and son and came to Sarajevo, where his sister has an apartment and where, he thought, he would be able to stay until the situation had calmed and he could go home. His was the last bus from Goražde to Sarajevo in April last year. It was on that journey, he says, that he realized the nature and scale of the crime that was taking place. 'I looked out of the window of the bus,' he said, 'and everywhere I saw the flags and symbols of the Serbian nation, and I knew that our homeland was being stolen from us; that on the land which we shared with them for generations, on which we had lived together, there was no longer room for us.' Suad's parents never made it. His father was killed when the town fell, shot according to others who escaped, along with some of his neighbours. A Muslim neighbour who later fled to Bosnian government-held territory and then to Sarajevo came looking for Suad to break the news. 'They made me dig your father's grave,' he told Saud. 'I thought I would be killed too, but they let me go.'

Suad, and Foča generally, illustrate eloquently the crime on which the republic of Srpska has been founded. The Bosnian government, defeated in war and politically collapsing, wants part of the municipality of Foča back. 'If you are forcing us to accept ethnic partition,' they have told the peace mediators in Geneva, 'then at least let us have it consistently applied so that those areas that had a Muslim majority before all this began come within the Muslim republic.' But the demand has fallen on deaf ears. No part of Foča will ever be returned to the sovereignty of the Bosnian government, and the Muslims will not go home. Foča is part of a new republic, whose very name suggests ethnic purity and which one day will rejoin Serbia and Montenegro in a new Yugoslav federation.

The logic of the Geneva peace process is that the world will recognize, despite saying that it does not, that powerful armies do have the right to change borders by force. In all wars, as the deputy mayor of Foča observed, there is no right or wrong; there are only winners and losers.

PEACE TRAIN

MISHA GLENNY   KRAKOW   16 OCTOBER 1993

The nationalist tensions that wrought so much havoc in the former Yugoslavia and elsewhere in eastern Europe were the subject of a conference which took place in an extraordinary location – aboard a train which had once served as the official means of transport of Janos Kadar, the former communist leader of Hungary.

The train emerged from the fog and pulled into Krakow Central Station with a deliberate grace. The fog was provided by nature in deference to the rich tradition of rail imagery which is dotted around central and east European literature and history, from *Anna Karenina* via Lenin's journey in a sealed train across Germany to *The Third Man*. In contrast to the dilapidated rolling stock of Polish railways, however, Janos Kadar's old train had been given a lick of bright blue paint and was adorned with the flags of the participants of Conference Express. The *chef du train*, turned out in a smart navy-blue uniform, was determined to offer the same high quality of service to the delegates and co-chairmen of the conference as he had done for many years to Kadar himself.

The former defence secretary and chancellor of the exchequer, Lord Healey, had flown to Krakow to launch the conference. With the weight of decades of diplomatic experience behind him, he proffered his advice to the two co-chairmen, myself and Arne-Olav Brundtland, who doubles as the Norwegian prime minister's husband in his spare time. 'Let the delegates have their say,' intoned Lord Healey gravely, 'and then get them to sign the set of principles which you will have written yourselves.' This is sound advice when you are dealing with a bundle of people from the former Yugoslavia and a nexus of Romanians, Hungarians and Slovaks who are unlikely to see eye-to-eye on a great deal.

The news on the eve of the conference was ominous. Three delegates from the former Yugoslavia cancelled or simply failed to show up. Slobodan Milošević's wife, Mirjana Marković, had apparently slumped into one of her periodical clinical depressions. Mohammed Filipović, the most flamboyant member of the Bosnian delegation to the Geneva talks, was stranded in Sarajevo as the United Nations would not give him permission to get a flight out of the besieged Bosnian capital. Božo Kovačević, the vice-president of Croatia's leading opposition party, pulled out in a panic, saying he must stay in Zagreb to save Croatian democracy. One cynical conference official muttered, 'I didn't know there was such a thing to save.' The happiest delegate of all, with his Švejk-like moustache and expanding beer-gut, was Jiří Dienstbier, the former foreign minister of former Czechoslovakia, as he describes himself. As the senior delegate, he had been alloted Kadar's personal compartment which, although hardly palatial, did have some impressively exclusive toilet facilities.

Holding a conference with a group of fractious delegates is difficult enough under the best of circumstances. But trying to maintain order with the train rolling from side to side and normal movement made virtually impossible by dint of two camera crews and three extra diesel generators brought in to power the equipment was an experience that the co-chairmen will never forget. Along the way we stopped at some of the most unstable points on the national fault-lines along which we were travelling.

There was Sahy, a Hungarian village in southern Slovakia where the local population claim that the Slovak authorities are trampling on their right to use Hungarian in public. But the most devastating experience of all was a visit to a Bosnian refugee camp in southern Hungary. I have talked to dozens, if not hundreds, of refugees from Croatia and Bosnia, yet each time there is no reduction in pain. The Hungarian authorities, themselves strapped for cash, have clearly done all they can to make these blighted people feel welcome. The camp was clean and efficient, but how long can anyone bear sleeping twelve or fifteen to a room the size of an average living room? 'There is no future for us and our children, there is only a black hole,' said Amira, a refugee from Tešanj, as she clutched her baby, which was born six months ago into a social void. More than anything, Amira's words reminded the conference that there was serious business to get through. Fundamental differences emerged in the discussions. Most delegates insisted that only a thorough implementation of minority rights could stop the drift into armed conflict in the various regions of Eastern Europe. Jiří Dienstbier, however, vigorously opposed this, arguing that only universal rights, guaranteed to all citizens, could ensure stability. 'If you start singling out people for special treatment or rights, you are going down a nationalist road to hell,' he warned. Given the rich mix of representatives from the former Yugoslavia, it was not surprising that a fairly vociferous argument flared up between them. At one point it looked very serious, but the co-chairmen steered the dispute through the rocky terrain. In the end, Lord Healey's advice uppermost in their minds, they succeeded in getting nine signatures on the statement of principles just as the train was drawing in majestically to Budapest's Western station.

Predictably, the conclusions of the conference were not what you would describe as optimistic. To sum it up in a few words, the conference concluded: 'We are in a mess in eastern Europe and something must be done about it pretty damn quick.' I do not think there was a single person on that train who believed that anything would be done about it.

NUCLEAR UKRAINE

MISHA GLENNY   KIEV   9 DECEMBER 1993

Russia's western neighbour, Ukraine, continued to be a cause for concern, in both Washington and Moscow, because of the presence of nuclear weapons on its soil. Leonid Kravchuk's Party of Power was duly voted out, but Ukraine continued to maintain that it would not dismantle its nuclear arsenal until it had been sufficiently compensated.

'Do you have any money?' 'No, I do not have any money.' 'Can you give me some money?' 'No, you cannot have any money.' It was the BBC's English course blaring out of the car radio that alerted me to the most fundamental fact of Ukrainian life as our hired Volga lurched towards Kiev from the airport, Borispil. Nobody has any money in Ukraine, and unfortunately that includes the government. Ordinary folk in Europe's fourth most populous, but scarcely heard of, country are faced with little alternative this winter; they scrape together the most meagre victuals and they huddle in their coats when the heating is turned off. Some people living in high-rise buildings on the endless housing estates of Kiev resort to extraordinary measures. On the fifth floor of one block, I knocked on a door. 'Maa, Maa,' came the reply. The door opened slowly to reveal Whitey, Blackie and three other goats who live there in the tiny entrance hall. 'I like the milk,' said Piotr, the urban farmer, 'and they make good meat.' Some of his neighbours are less than convinced. The day before I went to visit, the entire plumbing system of the high-rise broke down because goat droppings did not agree with it.

The government resorts to one or two other methods to stay alive. As one sceptical American observer in Ukraine told me: 'The government sees it is short of x million dollars. It observes that some of the delicate private banks which have emerged over the past two years have got that x million dollars. It does not ask the banks if it may borrow that money, it passes an emergency financial decree ordering them to hand over half of what they have carefully saved and throws them a bunch of worthless coupons instead.'

Ever since the Ukrainians threw off the Soviet yoke, the Party of Power, as the ruling élite in the capital Kiev is sinisterly known, has been doing everything to stop the reform of this creaking but potentially rich economy. It has also told the Russians to take a hike, and this has resulted in the virtual breakdown of much of the country's industry. The Russians were, of course, very unhappy at the unfriendly attitude taken by their former compatriots and new neighbours. So they responded by saying: 'Well, if that's the way you feel about it, you can start paying the full whack for our oil and gas which you use so much of. Put that in your pipe and smoke it!'

Ukraine suffers as a result, but adversity does not bring the people together. This country, which has a proud sense of its own history, has never experienced stable independence and Ukrainians are having enormous difficulty finding their identity. In the west, the Catholic Ukrainians dream of the revival of the Austro-Hungarian empire and their old connections with German culture. In the densely populated east, which is characterized by vast Leninist industries, most Ukrainians speak Russian and are known as Sovietized Ukrainians. There is also a huge Russian minority here, with whom the local Ukrainians rub along very happily. In the middle is Kiev, trying to pull together these two irreconcilable Ukrainian identities whilst simultaneously trying to accumulate as much power as possible at the expense of the regions.

Throw in several hundred decaying nuclear warheads and perhaps it becomes clearer why we should take Ukraine and its problems more seriously. The Russians certainly do and, with the full support of the United States, Russian diplomacy regularly growls at Kiev that it must give up the weapons. And of course what does Kiev say but 'Can you give me some money?' The Party of Power is using the presence of these weapons to try to extract money from the West to prop up an economy which the government itself has gutted. Not one person I spoke to in Ukraine had a good word to say about the government. It is universally hated, but clings stubbornly on to power. Now, contrary to their reputation, Ukrainians are a docile lot and it will take much to get them out onto the streets. But I have a sneaking suspicion that the Party of Power is going to crumble soon. When it does, the West and Russia must address Ukrainian concerns as quickly as possible so that this nuclear nonsense may be stopped once and for all.

WHERE THERE'S A WILL

KEVIN CONNOLLY   MOSCOW
9 DECEMBER 1993

Russia held its first parliamentary elections since the October Revolution seventy-six years earlier. But many eyes were fixed on another big vote, the race for the presidency, to be played out in 1996.

It is a bit like the beginning of one of those comforting old murder novels where the younger generation, greedy and mutually suspicious, gathers at the family mansion. No one, of course, knows the details of the will. After all, if they did, half the cast would not have turned up. And the blustering, irascible, unpredictable patriarch shows, as is traditional in such stories, disconcerting and inconvenient signs of good health. The inheritance in this case is the Russian presidency; the head of the household, Boris Yeltsin; the rambling, Gothic family pile, the Kremlin. Once you have decided on the casting, the rest of the parable is relatively straightforward. The part of the dry, correct, rather dull family solicitor, in the suit that made its first appearance at its owner's wedding long ago, must go to the prime minister, Viktor Chernomyrdin. But is there a glint of ambition behind those old-fashioned spectacles? It is galling, after all, to see the inheritance you have helped to shape handed on to a young man who you feel might not be quite as ready for it as you are yourself.

As for the parts of the three sons: first, I think, Yegor Gaidar, minister for economics, deputy prime minister and the kind of person, you cannot help thinking, who always had his hand up with the answer before the teacher had got the whole question out. He is tubby but curiously youthful, and it is just possible that the head of the family might fear he would be too ready to risk the already rapidly dwindling family fortunes on investment schemes dreamt up by his flashy friends from the West. The part of the middle son has to go to another deputy prime minister, Sergei Shakhrai, who has the dependable but unexciting good looks of a junior detective from a quiet rural beat. He certainly has an engaging honesty, and a slightly less engaging way of telling you about it himself. However, he has incurred the wrath of the current head of the family by being just a little too open about his intention of taking over one day. When you are in charge it may well do you good to dwell from time to time on your own mortality, but you are most unlikely to acquire a taste for listening to others dwelling on it in public. So worthy Sergei is unlikely to inherit. Still more unlikely to succeed, perhaps, is the third son, Grigory Yavlinsky; once a slightly scruffy academic, he has recently acquired a certain brittle glamour, and the sort of suit and haircut you would expect to see being worn on the sleeve of a 1970s easy-listening record. But he is something of an outsider, too ready to be scathing in front of strangers about the current incumbent's stewardship of the family fortunes.

Moving mysteriously around the estate, and no doubt thinking dark, private thoughts about the three sons, are the faithful family retainers: Gennady Burbulis, a one-time academic, and Mikhail Poltoranin, a former newspaper editor. Faintly sinister, they owe their undeniable power behind the throne to their loyalty to the current head of the Russian political family. There can be few butlers in such positions, knowing how heavily their advice has been relied on, who have not toyed with the pleasing fantasy that they might themselves inherit the legacy they have toiled so industriously to protect. But what should they do in the meantime? Gamble everything on trying to turn the boss against all the young pretenders, or cultivate one of them, and hope that their influence will be enough to swing the final decision their way? These are difficult parts, calling for characters capable of being, by turns, conciliatory, confrontational, devious and manipulative – and they are parts the two men are handsomely equipped to play. And, of course, there are the characters beyond the immediate family circle; like the wild, distant cousin, Vladimir Zhirinovsky, with the air of a night-club bouncer going before a parole hearing. He holds a variety of extreme views on practically everything, ranging from the merely eccentric through the dislikeable to the dangerous. But he insists that he could be head of the family one day, and claims that many of its most important members secretly share at least some of his opinions.

And, finally, presiding over the gathering, there is Boris Yeltsin. He is wearying of responsibility now, he says, but remains apparently convinced that for the moment he must stay in charge. He has spoken publicly about the day when, eventually, he will step down, but if he is conscious of the frantic manoeuvring going on around him, he shows little sign of it. This is, of course, merely the opening chapter in the drama. But, like all the best opening chapters, it concludes with a hint of further drama still to come. The head of the family has discussed the question of who will follow him, but he has also given a cryptic warning to the pretenders that it will be someone who has not yet put himself forward, setting the stage for a mystery character to appear unannounced. Don't miss the next instalment.

THE REINVENTION OF MR ZHIRINOVSKY

KEVIN CONNOLLY   MOSCOW
16 DECEMBER 1993

The election to the Russian parliament of the hardliner Vladimir Zhirinovsky caused shockwaves around the world. He was, after all, the man who had threatened nuclear strikes against Japan and Germany and wanted to restore the borders of the old Soviet Union.

The candidate was getting restless. In his crumpled suit, his tie carelessly knotted under the open collar of his shirt and his eyes tired and drained of life by the strain of the campaign, he shifted uncomfortably in a solid-looking swivel chair. A colourful teddy bear had slipped drunkenly at an uncomfortable angle between two piles of books on a table behind him. A war veteran shuffled in to offer his support. It was a big day for him, and he had pinned his carefully cleaned medals on the front of his grubby, ill-fitting overcoat. Mr Zhirinovsky favoured him with one of those quick but intimate double-handed handshakes that I suppose all good politicians must practise in private, and sat down again. He reached down to a switch located somewhere at ankle height behind him, turning off the harsh overhead fluorescent light and turning on a floodlight focused squarely on his chair. Mr Zhirinovsky is a quick-witted lawyer – at least from the point of view of speed and convenience – and a delight to interview.

Yes, he conceded politely, he did have presidential ambitions, and when Boris Yeltsin was off the scene he didn't believe anyone would have a chance of beating him. The youthful economic liberals who ran Mr Yeltsin's painfully unpopular reform programme might then

79

learn the lesson that the more you impoverish people, the less they are likely to vote for you. He did not, however, want to use force to restore the borders of the old Soviet Union. That would not be necessary. 'Cut off their subsidized oil and electricity,' he said, 'and they'll be back on their knees begging for Moscow to rule them again.' With the help of a prop, he dismissed the idea of Ukrainian independence. 'We're both sitting at my desk,' he said. 'I'm Russia and I'm in the middle. You're Ukraine and you're at the edge. But it's still only one table and it's still mine.' The thorny subject of prejudice was similarly addressed. 'As a people,' he said, 'the Jews should be proud; they have a great culture.' But he couldn't help adding: 'They are themselves responsible for the existence of anti-Semitism.' And so it goes on. Through carefully phrased denials of things he is said to have said, and light-hearted evasions of things he is thought to have thought, Mr Zhirinovsky is reinventing himself.

It is not an easy process, and it is not going any more smoothly for Mr Zhirinovsky than it tends to for other extremists in the same position. Asked why he has been known to surround himself with men in black suits and mirror sunglasses, he was outraged. 'Only one of the men you saw was wearing sunglasses,' he argued indignantly, 'and he has something wrong with his eyes.' Questioned about his views on America, he said generously that he was worried that the country was on the point of disintegration. But, gracious towards an old adversary, he said he would take no pleasure in California's coming food shortages or, indeed, in the creation of the breakaway negro republic of South Miami.

You can find out more, of course, by reading Mr Zhirinovsky's book, *The Last Push Southwards*, which might be summed up as an explanation of how Russia's destiny is to bring peace to the whole world by invading, subjugating, dominating or threatening half the countries that make it up. Only 143 pages long, it manages to strike an oddly colourful note, with weary but victorious Russian soldiers washing their boots in the Mediterranean Sea and the Indian Ocean. The underlying tone, however, is apocalyptic, with a mighty Russia arising in the nick of time to save a vaguely defined culture he believes to be under threat from a hostile but improbable coalition that includes Finland, China, Japan, Turkey, most of the Middle East, and one or two others I can't remember. I can't remember either exactly how war breaks out, but with Mr Zhirinovsky the arch Russian nationalist at the typewriter, there can be no doubt as to how it ends.

And this, remember, is the new, reasonable Mr Zhirinovsky. It is not the Mr Zhirinovsky who sent volunteers to fight for Iraq in the Gulf War – that was a cultural exchange, he now says – or the man who once promised the world more Hiroshimas and Nagasakis. But curiously, unless you live in one of the countries deemed to be in Russia's path, the impression you carry away from the book is of an awkward and intelligent man whose unhappy personality has been the catalyst for the conversion of a ragbag of faintly weird geo-political theories into a genuinely dangerous set of policies. He writes of feeling unwanted as a child, unloved at home, unpopular at school. He would have preferred, he says, to have poured his energy into love, sex or even friendship rather than politics. When he came to Moscow as a young student, his early experiences with girls, he adds with disconcerting directness, were unsuccessful. This is uncomfortable reading, and more uncomfortable still is the knowledge that the bizarre linking of ideas which lies behind it is still there. This is, after all, the man who promised to give Russia an orgasm next year.

It may all sound inexpressibly odd from the outside that Mr Zhirinovsky has been converted by the Russian electorate from demagogic clown to fascist president-in-waiting in just a few days, but the truth is not surprising. He has ignored, by and large, the practical, political and economic costs of Soviet collapse and concentrated on the profound sense of hurt and loss, almost grief, that many Russians feel about it. They have been mourning lost greatness and he, after mourning with them, now promises to restore it. In this odd, volatile and dangerous man Russia has found, if not a hero of the hour, then at least a figure to match these dangerous and depressing times. Shrewd, clever and ambitious, he now wants to be president. It is possible we will all pay a high price for the fact that no one at school wanted to speak to Vladimir Zhirinovsky.

JOIN THE CLUB

TIM WHEWELL   MOSCOW   23 DECEMBER 1993

The BBC's Moscow bureau finally moved from old, cramped quarters in a Stalin-era apartment block to a purpose-built suite in a new, American-run hotel. When our former Moscow Correspondent returned to the city, he was struck by the contrast between the BBC's new home and the railway station opposite, which had become a haven for Moscow's poor and dispossessed.

What I noticed first were the tracksuits – the woolly blue tracksuit tops worn in place of a shirt under old, shiny jackets. Twelve years ago, when I first lived in the Soviet Union, those tops were the most modern thing you could buy in state clothes shops. Every second person seemed to sport the extraordinary combination of blue nylon and brown polyester. When I worked in Moscow during the years of Mr Gorbachev's reforms, it seemed to me that Russians were gradually becoming better dressed – by the time I left, few Muscovites seemed to lack a pair of Wranglers or Levis. But when you return to Russia you're more conscious of what hasn't changed, and it turns out that the blue tracksuits are still there, especially around the Kiev railway station.

Not only the tracksuits, but all the poverty and hopelessness they seemed to symbolize are still in evidence: a pair of recent drinking partners inching towards a fight in one entrance to the station, a forlorn family sprawled over a pile of sack-covered bundles in another, and everywhere that smell composed of dust, sweat, urine, stale beer, and perhaps boiled frankfurters. The Kiev station and its milling mass of insulted and humiliated humanity has not changed that much with the years, but I had forgotten what it was like. Now, coming back, I confronted the scene every day on my way to work in the huge concrete fortress known as the Slavyanskaya Hotel. From station to hotel I had to cross not just a street, but a barrier between unconnected worlds. Once through the hotel's succession of plate-glass doors, you find yourself on an expanse of thick carpet where waiters in black bow-ties bob and weave between deep leather armchairs. There is a shopping mall, a health club, a Viennese-style pavement café and Moscow's only truly authentic American steak-house. Upstairs a business area looks as though it's been filled by a Hollywood casting agent with men in striped shirts and braces and mini-skirted Russian interpreters perched professionally on the arms of sofas.

Of course, international hotels all over the world share the same anonymous culture – but few can take quite so little from their host country. You can't buy a Russian newspaper without returning to the maelstrom of the Kiev station. You can get Russian television in your room – although that fact is not advertised – on about channel 26, far behind CNN, the BBC and the continuous soft porn. Receptionists and waiters will automatically address you in English. And even if you happen to be Russian there's not much point in standing on your dignity, because if you're going for the hotel's most popular lunchtime snack, the club sandwich, you'll still be reduced to saying, 'Klubny sendvich, pozhaluista.'

I confess I have a problem with the club sandwich. I can't work out what club could have devised it, unless it was the club of people with strangely shaped mouths. But my problem is compounded in Moscow by embarrassment in front of Russians who might think Westerners regularly waste their time cutting toast into tiny triangles and threading it onto a stick before taking it off again so that the bits of chicken and turkey can fall into your lap anyway. Of course, there were once Russian club sandwiches. In one pre-revolutionary Moscow tavern merchants used to conduct business over a twelve-storey pie, with everything from fish liver at the top to bone marrow in black butter at the bottom. But that was more substantial than what's now offered at the Hotel Slavyanskaya and ... it was Russian. Indeed, according to memoirs from the time, one of the millionaires who were most fond of it used to say: 'Don't give me any of those folies-jolies and fricory-chicories. We eat Russian, and we're never ill.'

In those days, Russian capitalism was heavily influenced by tradi-tional merchant culture. This time round, everything seems to be imported. A couple of years ago, in an echo of the pie-loving merchant, the then vice-president, Alexander Rutskoi, launched an extraordinary public attack on Moscow's most popular tourist attraction after the Kremlin and Red Square: the McDonald's hamburger restaurant. People didn't go to McDonald's to fill their bellies, he said, but to take communion at the altar of Western values. And in what sense were hamburgers superior to Russian fish patties, which you couldn't get for love or money?

We may never know how Mr Rutskoi would have fared at the ballot box, because he made a grave mistake in trying to lead an armed revolt in October and was sent to Moscow's most secure gaol. But another Russian nationalist who cleverly stayed out of that fray, Vladimir Zhirinovsky, won millions of votes in elections this month, and those votes didn't come just from the poor, but from people who have done well for themselves in the last few years. Why? Because, as one acquaintance in the latter category put it, Mr Zhirinovsky 'made Russians feel better about themselves'.

What does the Hotel Slavyanskaya have that's Russian? It has its staff – well paid by local standards, with an obvious stake in reform, but working in an atmosphere that seems to stress the superiority of foreign culture. I wouldn't be surprised if some of those in bow-ties on one side of the glass doors voted the same way as those in blue tracksuits on the other.

SHATTERED FRIENDSHIPS

ALLAN LITTLE   EDINBURGH   1 JANUARY 1994

1993 was another bloody year for Bosnia and its capital, Sarajevo. It was a year in which the international community had to come to terms with the de facto partition of the country and the prospect of the division of Sarajevo itself along ethnic lines. It was a partition that would erect permanent barriers between people who were once the closest of friends.

She begins her letter to her son with three words that have talons to rip out your heart. She is stuck in Sarajevo, a middle-aged, middle-class widow, educated, urbane, a Sarajevan in all senses, and her son is here, in Edinburgh. He might as well be on another planet for all the contact he has with her, and with everything that has ever really mattered to him. It has been many weeks since he has had news from his home town and, one day just before Christmas, a letter arrives, smuggled out of the city by a departing journalist. He tears it open, and the first three words do, indeed, tear out his heart: 'My Dear Child.' The greeting is so heavy with sorrow and longing, a mother reaching out across an impossible divide to the son she cannot embrace and from whom, she now fears, she may be separated for ever, that for a moment he cannot bring himself to read further. He lifts his head from the page and says, 'No matter how strong I think I have become, it only takes a piece of paper to break me.'

With the perspective that the New Year gives, one story stands out in sharp relief in my mind. It is the story of a coincidence not so much remarkable as revealing, a story that speaks eloquently about the fate of Sarajevo, and of Bosnia, and, in a way, of the complicity of an international community acting in the name of us all. It began in April. We were in a fifth-floor flat in the besieged Bosnian capital, and I was interviewing the three young men who lived there. It was a flat like any shared student flat anywhere in Europe, except that the glass blown out of its window frames had been replaced by plastic sheeting supplied by the humanitarian agencies. These three were, it turned out, all twenty-two years old, all fighting in the Bosnian army, fighting to lift the Serb-imposed siege of Sarajevo and to liberate what they all saw as the occupied areas of their country. They were all ethnic Serbs. The Bosnian army was then, and in Sarajevo remains, not Muslim but multi-ethnic. This was their story.

On 2 May 1992, the Bosnian Serb army and the Yugoslav federal army had launched a major offensive – their only serious effort to date to capture the heart of the city. The suburb of Grbavica, where these three lived with their families, fell overnight. A week later, on 9 May, a notice appeared in the lobby of every apartment block instructing all Serb men between the ages of eighteen and fifty-five to report for military service within a week. The next day, Zoran decided to leave. 'The front lines were still shifting,' he said. 'It still wasn't clear who was in control. I took the decision to run across the river. The other two were leaning out of the window of their own building and I signalled to them that I was going to the other side. They followed the same day. None of us wanted to fire on our own city, against our own people.'

The three had been friends since primary school, from the age of seven. Their principal sadness was that the fourth member of their gang, Braco, had stayed behind. Braco's mother was a widow and he was an only child; he had decided, when his friends left, not to leave her. He was now in the opposing army, a fighter in the besieging force. Their best friend had become their mortal enemy, but they did not see it this way. They spoke about him with affection and loyalty. He had been the clown of the group, the butt of their jokes, principally because of his poor eyesight and thick glasses, and from the age of seven he had been known by a nickname that was a play on the Serbo-Croat word for spectacles. The war, they insisted, would not change their friendship. They would be together again when this was all over. That, they said, was the strength of Sarajevo, and it would survive.

Four months later I went to Grbavica, to the Serb-held suburb from which the three had fled, leaving their friend Braco to join the enemy army. Grbavica is a tongue of territory that juts into the heart of the city. The river forms the front line, and from an apartment block on the water's edge, I noted that we were no more than three hundred yards from the flat, on the other side of the line, in which I had interviewed them. Those who still live here, mostly but not exclusively Serbs, are as much at risk from sniper fire and shelling as their former neighbours in the besieged city that is so near and so visible.

We were shown around the district by a young man wearing the uniform of the Bosnian Serb army and bearing the insignia of the White Eagles, a Serb nationalist emblem that still strikes fear into the hearts of those Muslims who were forced to leave their homes in the first, ferocious days of ethnic cleansing. He took us back to his home, a flat on the riverside in a building two sides of which were uninhabitable because they were exposed to Bosnian army gun positions only a hundred yards away. 'This is sovereign Serb territory,' he insisted. 'When the war is won, we will need a wall through the heart of Sarajevo, for the protection of the Serbian people. We are building our own state in Bosnia, and we will have to defend it.' I asked him if he had seen much military action himself. 'I'm not much of a fighter,' he confessed. 'My eyesight is too poor for the front line. I'm a radio operator really.'

Suddenly, it struck me. This was Braco, the fourth member of the gang, and the memory of his three friends and their tenacious loyalty to the one who had stayed behind came flooding back. 'I know who you are,' I said, 'you're Braco.' I told him I knew his friends, that they were alive and well, and that they had spoken warmly of him and wanted to see him again. Stunned is not a word that captures his reaction. It was as though I had punched him in the stomach: he was speechless. 'Come with me,' he said. We climbed to the fourteenth floor of the apartment block and went into a flat that had been destroyed by rocket fire. 'This is where my mother and I lived. We moved out when the place was hit. We moved three floors down to a flat that used to belong to a Muslim neighbour, a doctor. He and his family left at the start of the war.'

We went into an adjoining room. All the furniture had been removed, apart from one small couch. On the couch there was a bundle of letters and postcards, tied together with a green ribbon. He picked them up. 'These are the letters those three wrote to me when they were away doing their national service in 1990,' he said. Under his breath he cursed the war and the division of Sarajevo he had been advocating enthusiastically only a few minutes earlier.

I told him I would see his friends soon, and said he should record a message to them on my tape-recorder. He agreed, and I switched it on. He spoke for a few seconds, a string of greetings: 'Hi there, this is Braco. How are you? Take care. Look after yourselves.' Then he told me he had something else to say. I switched it back on. 'This is for all three of you,' he said. 'I still love you, all of you. That's it.'

I went to see the other three the next day in the flat just three hundred yards from where their enemy-friend had shown me the letters. Zoran's physical and mental condition had deteriorated in the months since I had last seen him. His father, at fifty-nine, had been drafted into the Bosnian Serb army. The war had now pitted father against son. His parents, he had discovered, had, earlier in the year, been informed by the Bosnian Serb authorities that he, Zoran, had been killed in battle and that arrangements were being made to recover his body. Only when the body exchange had taken place did the family discover that he was not, after all, among the dead. But for three days they had been receiving condolences from relatives and friends. 'These days,' said Zoran, 'I cannot sleep at night without enough tranquillizers to stun a horse.' He was no longer enthusiastic about the spirit of Sarajevo. 'We will be friends again,' he said, 'but they, on that side, will never understand what their shells have done to this city.'

Bosnia was partitioned in 1993; 1994 will be the year of the partition of Sarajevo. The Bosnian Serb leaders want the city divided, and they have learned that the world, eventually, lets them have what they want. The lesson is that, in the post-Cold War world, to build a state you need neither a sound argument nor a just case, but a strong army. Zoran knows now that he will only ever see his friend again if they both leave Bosnia, and former Yugoslavia, altogether. The spirit of Sarajevo that he trumpeted so confidently in the spring has been killed, and those who hated its multiculturalism, its tolerance, its muddled ethnic impurity, have won the war.

SHOPPING WITH MR BERLUSCONI

MATT FREI   ROME   22 JANUARY 1994

As Italian politicians dropped one after another in the great clean-out of corruption from the Italian establishment, one man emerged as a possible future leader. But would the country really elect a former cruise-ship crooner to the job of prime minister of Italy?

When Roman generals returned to the capital from a successful battle and rode through the city in triumph, decorated by the Senate and hailed by the people, a man used to stand behind them on the chariot, and gently whisper into their ear: 'Remember you are not a God.' It struck me that Silvio Berlusconi, Italy's wealthiest media tycoon and its would-be leader, also needs one of those men. I had gone to Turin for the opening of the country's biggest hypermarket, a consumer Eden located in a vast shopping mall, marooned in the middle of a never-ending building site. The streets had been cordoned off by policemen, and blue lights flashed eerily through the thick freezing fog. But Mr Berlusconi was not even coming by road – he prefers helicopters. When he finally landed, an entourage of more than a dozen bodyguards with earpieces appeared with him out of the fog, as well as a retinue of bag-carriers, advisers and beautiful secretaries with clipboards. I had to remind myself that Mr Berlusconi was not being inaugurated as president of Italy, although he would very much like to be one day, but was merely opening a supermarket, albeit a very big one.

Mr Berlusconi, who owns three television stations, several pub-lishing houses, newspapers and magazines, controls one-third of all advertising in Italy, feeds millions of Italians with his supermarkets, houses tens of thousands in the futuristic satellite cities he has built, and happens to own AC Milan, the current football champions. This same Berlusconi can be no more than five and a half feet tall, yet he is compelling to look at, and clearly expects you to look at him. His skin has a deep, almost orange, tan that looks extraterrestrial at this time of year. His teeth are perfectly shaped, white and always visible, thanks to a permanent smile. Before he became a media mogul and football tycoon, Mr Berlusconi worked as a night-club crooner on Italian cruise-ships. He still sways gently when he walks, as if steadying himself deftly on a slippery stage during high seas. The former entertainer has lost none of his old touch. As he inspected a formation of giggling cashier girls in pink uniforms and handled a huge salami from the sausage stand, I thought for a moment that he might break into song. Under the watchful eye of his bodyguards he hugged, kissed and patted his way from frozen foods to fresh fish and ended up in confectionery, standing underneath a ceiling dripping with red, heart-shaped balloons. The ghost of Federico Fellini was with us.

Mr Berlusconi had made a very simple calculation. The Italians, he told himself, ate his food, watched his television channels with their low-fibre diet of game shows and soft porn, and loved his football team. Surely they would also worship him if he went into politics. He may be right. According to one opinion poll he is more popular than Jesus Christ among nine- to thirteen-year-olds. His ratings amongst Italians of voting age are not bad, either. He is one of the few business tycoons not to be personally embroiled in the corruption scandal that has brought down so many politicians and ruined so many business dynasties. Too good to be true, say the sceptics, especially since Mr Berlusconi was a close personal friend of the former prime minister Bettino Craxi, who is up to his neck in charges. Mr Berlusconi benefited enormously from the redrafting of a broadcasting law that allowed him alone to own three television channels, attracting half the country's viewers.

But, so far at least, Berlusconi is untainted, and that is saying a lot in Italy these days. His political philosophy, inspired by his two great heroes Ronald Reagan and Lady Thatcher, is conservative, free-market and so anti-left you would think the Cold War was still in full swing. He has offered to save Italy from the red peril of a left-wing alliance, dominated by the former communists. He proposes to do this with what he calls 'a Liberal-Democratic alliance of centre and right-wing parties'. He fears that if the right does not get its act together, its candidates will be competing against each other in Italy's new British-style, one-member constituencies. His fears are completely justified.

But despite his success with the consumer, Mr Berlusconi has had great difficulty in finding political partners. The tycoon's supporters will tell you that this is because their idol is too big for the small men of Italian politics to handle. His critics say it is because Berlusconi has an ego that is too big for anyone to handle, even himself. Of course he isn't just relying on others; he has started his own party, called Forza Italia. This translates as 'Go for it, Italy'. Anyone can join: you dial a special number advertised on one of Berlusconi's channels, and a soft voice tells you where to sign up. If you want to become a grass-roots activist you can pay 500,000 lire, about £200. This buys you a Forza Italia Campaign Kit, including a briefcase, with leaflets, T-shirts, stickers, badges, a tie, handkerchiefs and, oddly enough, a whistle. Silvio Berlusconi has already hand-picked scores of candidates, many from the worlds of entertainment and sport.

Commentators are in two minds about whether these American-style feel-good PR tactics will work in the tangled forests of Italian politics. Some say you can not pick and choose a party like a football team. Others believe that slick Silvio is just the ticket. There remains, however, the minor matter of whether it is ethical for the owner of three television channels, whose news broadcasts are perceptibly slanted in favour of their owner, to go into politics. And there is the major matter of the health of Berlusconi's empire: the tycoon has debts of almost £2 billion, and is said to have been side-lined in his own business by a trouble-shooter appointed by the creditor banks. Despite the thousands of Forza Italia briefcases that are travelling up and down the country, despite the brand-new, expensively furnished party headquarters, and despite the fact that so many Italians clearly want a strong but honest leader, Mr Berlusconi may not be the right man for the job. He may opt out – but that would be extraordinary for a man with an ego of his size.

MARKETPLACE MASSACRE

PAUL ADAMS   SARAJEVO   5 FEBRUARY 1994

The event that triggered action from the international community and the end of the siege of Sarajevo was the bomb attack on the city's market-place on 5 February. More than sixty people lost their lives.

I saw the market-place twice on Saturday. At about eleven o' clock I was driving back from the Jewish Community Centre, having just watched some three hundred people getting ready to leave Sarajevo. They sat patiently in their buses, Jews and non-Jews gazing out at the city they love, but which has been the scene of such unbearable suffering. I spoke to Rahela, a Jew who was leaving with her Muslim husband Atef. They were bound for Israel to join two young sons who had left the city almost two years before, when the war began. Rahela was leaving with a heavy heart and doubted that she would ever be back; she had already seen too much. We left the convoy with its hopeful, tearful passengers and turned back to the Holiday Inn, crossing the river and driving through the heart of the old city, where the battered architecture still speaks eloquently of Sarajevo's complex heritage. As we neared the market we slowed to a crawl, our lumbering armoured Land-Rover suddenly inappropriate as we made our way gingerly through the packed streets. It seemed as if everyone had come downtown to mingle, to remind themselves what it feels like to be in the midst of a milling crowd on a Saturday morning. Much of the time Sarajevo feels empty and, despite the gunfire, silent too. It seemed miraculous to see so many people out enjoying the sunshine, lingering on street corners, strolling in couples. To witness scenes like this in a city so preoccupied with the business of survival is to experience normality as if for the first time.

My visit has been full of such moments. One night it was the haunting sound of a lone clarinettist playing a Beatles tune somewhere in the dark of a labyrinthine bunker in the television station. Another time it was simply the sight of three apartment blocks ablaze with light standing out against the Stygian backdrop of a city largely without power. They looked like Christmas trees. The residents were making the most of a few hours of electricity and the sight of so many illuminated windows – utterly banal in any other city – was quite breathtaking. And so, in a way, was the scene at the market-place; I turned to my colleague and said how normal it all looked. Dina is from Sarajevo and has worked with the BBC for much of the war, and her pleasure in the scene was tempered by apprehension. One explosion, she said, would change all this.

Two hours later we were back at the market-place. It was all but deserted, with a few policemen shooing onlookers away. There were sirens and, from somewhere up the street, the sound of a woman wailing hysterically. Through the empty market-stalls we could see where the shell had landed – but, for a place where an act of such appalling butchery had just been committed, it seemed surprisingly undamaged. It was only later, when I saw the television pictures of indescribable pieces of human flesh being removed from the scene, that I realized just how the blast had been absorbed. They say that only five small pieces of shrapnel were recovered from the market-place; the rest found its mark.

After twenty-two months, the city of Sarajevo has become an emblem of siege, its battered skyline and blood-stained streets instantly recognizable around the world. It is a Stalingrad of the television age, but ten years ago this week, the city opened its doors to the athletes of the world and hosted one of the most successful Winter Olympics of recent times. Sarajevo was back on the map – famous for something other than the assassination of Archduke Ferdinand in 1914. But the Sarajevo of 1984 has been blasted to smithereens by the Bosnian Serbs, who seem intent on restoring the city's reputation as the cradle of conflagration. The international community has stood by and watched, allowing itself to view the siege of Sarajevo as somehow routine; even, in a perverse way, as necessary. Our inaction stems from a sneaking belief that what is going on here is inevitable, that this is what occasionally happens to cities and peoples whose hour on the stage of history has run out. At a time when the citizens of this country are being picked off by snipers and blown up by shells in a long, protracted massacre it takes scenes of unspeakable carnage to jolt us into thinking whether, after all, we should try to stop it.

For the people of Sarajevo this realization comes far too late. They demand to know just how much of this we can bear to watch before we say that enough is enough. As journalists, descending like birds of prey on every private and public tragedy, we find ourselves being asked to account for the passivity of our governments. It is hard not to feel ashamed, or to avoid the feeling that it's adding insult to injury to attend a funeral. These people have long since concluded that they simply do not fit the international community's Balkan blueprint, and who can blame them? Isolated from the outside world, shot at every day from the hills, numbed by the boredom of the siege, their minds conceive sometimes fantastic theories to explain what is going on. One woman told me with utter conviction that she knew for a fact that United Nations officers brought their children on holiday to nearby Pale to play in the snow with little Serb children. It will take more than the threat of air strikes to begin to change her mind.

BACK TO BASICS – GREEK-STYLE

MALCOLM BRABANT   ATHENS
10 FEBRUARY 1994

The lifestyles of tens of thousands of Greeks changed when the government decided that all-night carousing was out and that night-clubs had to close by 3 a.m.

'It is a good thing that they will close so early. Now my wife will see more of me. I will have no excuse to stay out beyond half past three.' The ironic words came from a good friend of mine, a handsome womanizer of epic proportions whose head of prematurely grey hair and bloodshot eyes, wallowing in blackened bags, are badges of honour from a lifetime dedicated to nocturnal pleasures. Costas, for that is what I shall call him to save him from his wife's wrath, is the perfect spokesman for patrons of *bouzoukia* – overpriced night-clubs specializing in live, sentimental dance music dominated by the bouzouki, the eight-stringed mandolin-like instrument whose sound instantly conjures up images of Greece.

Every week for the past four years, Costas has said: 'Tonight, we go to *bouzoukia*, drink lots of whisky, and meet some bad women.' And every week for the past four years, apart from one or two occasions, I have said: 'No thanks, I would rather stay at home with a warm milky drink, a hot-water bottle and a copy of the New Testament.' But those handful of occasions when I have been seduced by the prospect of the best night of my life, plus a foray last week in the interests of research, give me the authority to say that the government's decision to order the early closure of night-clubs is a grievous assault on the essence of the Greek character, and another example of the all-pervasive influence of Brussels as it attempts to homogenize the nations of the European Union.

95

First, though, I must declare that apart from the sight of mini-skirted women gyrating provocatively on tables, I don't like *bouzoukia*. I think that by and large the music would struggle to make the preliminary rounds of the Eurovision Song Contest, and even then it would be 'Greece – nul points'. The volume is far too loud, which makes it impossible for me to convey in pigeon Greek and broken English to those gyrating, provocative dancers why they should prefer a wounderfully intelligent but impoverished *Anglos* to a Greek of similar podgy proportions, who has the advantage of a dockload of ships, an Aegean island and an amount of money similar to the gross domestic product of the United Arab Emirates at his disposal.

The way those podgy chaps of a certain age throw money around at *bouzoukia* means it's no surprise that they make such headway with impressionable girls young enough to be their mistresses. It's also no surprise that *bouzoukia* owners are putting up such a fight to enable them to stay open until the last dancer drops from exhaustion. These places, even the clubs in the poorest parts of town, are a licence to print money.

About two years ago, I went to one in Keseriani, a run-down working-class district on the outskirts of Athens. It was devoted to *rebetika* – acoustic bouzouki music redolent of the degenerate atmosphere of the opium and hashish dens of Asia Minor just after the First World War, before the Turks swept the Greeks out of towns like Smyrna, now Izmir, in population exchanges that followed a fierce ethnic conflict. I was with Costas and a woman from the Australian Embassy he was 'seeing' at the time, who had been trained at the Les Patterson school of diplomacy. We had gone to listen to a singer aged seventy or more who, it transpired, justified her legendary reputation. As befits a performer of her talent, she was showered with flowers after every song. Even in places like this, silver-foil trays containing five carnation heads cost about £3 a throw.

But the image which sticks out in my mind the most is of the man sitting at the table next to ours. He must have weighed twenty-five stone, give or take a few pounds. He was in the middle of a gargantuan meal, had done considerable damage to the bottle of whisky by his side, and was surrounded by hundreds of plates, piled up like the columns of a Greek temple around his table. He was too drunk, too bloated or simply too important to leap up on the stage and smash the plates in appreciation of the singer. He clicked his fingers. A waiter came over, and pushed the columns to the ground, where the plates cracked half-heartedly. The man then ordered several hundred more plates so that, presumably, the ritual could be repeated.

This lack of exuberance was all too much for Costas's Australian friend. Even someone as undiplomatic as I am has the common sense to recognize that it's just not *bouzoukia* etiquette to run over to a fat man's table, pinch about twenty plates, and smash them wildly, simply because he doesn't seem to know how to enjoy himself. But that's what she did. And it was made fairly clear to us by the management, and the fat man, that if he wanted to spend hundreds of pounds on expendable crockery to dispose of as he wished, then that was his business, and none of ours.

If the man had been a patron of one of the steel-and-glass music palaces lining Syngrou Avenue, which leads from the centre of Athens to the sea, or one of the plusher emporia next to the coast, the bill for his night's entertainment would have been far higher. It is not unusual to hear of people blowing thousands of pounds in these establishments buying flowers or champagne to compliment their favourite singers. To a conservative Western mind, the ceremony with the champagne is bemusing. Several times a night, a procession of waiters will carry crates of sparkling wine onto the stage and, with a great flourish, will pop open each bottle, raise it in the air next to the singer, and put it back in the box – full, minus a few bubbles. When the final bottle has been opened, the singer is handed a glass containing barely a mouthful. The waiter will point out the benefactor. The singer will raise the glass in his direction, raise it to her lips and, more often than not, not even take a sip.

Every time I see this happen I want to shout: 'For heaven's sake, it might be the rough stuff from the islands, but at least have the decency to have a taste.' What's worse is that the bubbly, all one hundred or so bottles, is then taken away and tipped down the drain or, more likely, re-corked and re-sold to another mug. Why do they do it, I ask? The only answer I ever get is that they have a Greek soul, and it gives them pleasure to spend money like that.

Bouzoukia embody the paradox of Greece, a country that's supposed to be broke, but whose people are loaded with cash. All this extravagance usually happens between two o'clock in the morning and dawn, when the overpriced whisky takes effect, which explains the intensity of the night-club owners' protests against early closure. But why has the government taken this unpopular stand? It claims that too many young people are spending too much time on the tiles, and not enough time at home or in the classroom. It also claims that under-age and excess drinking late at night has contributed to a rise in crime. Family and moral values are supposedly vanishing. But according to the more popular newspapers, these arguments are flawed, expecially as they come from a ruling party with a record of mistresses, irresponsibility and alleged corruption. 'What next,' they say, 'compulsory attendance at church?' In Greece, just as in England, 'back to basics' is a difficult message to swallow.

SARAJEVO: SHOULD WE INTERVENE?

PAUL REYNOLDS   LONDON   10 FEBRUARY 1994

After widespread television and radio coverage of the shelling of the marketplace in Sarajevo, there was a distinct shift in policy – the Bosnian Serbs were told by Nato to withdraw their heavy weapons or have them impounded by the UN. There was also a warning that further bombardment of the city would lead to retaliatory air strikes.

Last September in the classical elegance of the Travellers' Club in Pall Mall the foreign secretary, Mr Hurd, no mean traveller himself, took issue with another well-travelled group, reporters. 'Most of those who report for the BBC, *The Times*, the *Independent*, the *Guardian*,' he said, 'have been in different ways enthusiasts for pushing military intervention in Bosnia, whether by air or on the ground. They are the founder members of the "something must be done" school.'

The turnaround in British policy is quite astonishing. In the same speech, the foreign secretary said that the government had not been and was not willing to begin some form of military intervention which it judged useless, or simply because of pressure from the media. And yet that surely is what happened last Saturday: a Foreign Office official conceded that the marketplace explosion and the subsequent television coverage swung the balance in favour of tough action. The sad thing is that this could have been done earlier. From my own brief experience of Sarajevo during three weeks in December, I can say with confidence that the mortar in the central market was different only in scale from what goes on in the city every day. When I was there, a shell hit another market. Six people were killed, their blood staining the ground for hours afterwards. One unfortunate man lying in hospital had shrapnel in his chest. He had worked for years in a weapons factory at Vogošća, a town in Serb hands just north of Sarajevo. It was quite possible that his factory had made the shell that wounded him. Yet that incident passed off almost unnoticed by the outside world.

Day after day, the UN military spokesman gives figures for incoming shells. It is a rare day when the number falls below a hundred, and on two days when I was there it rose to well over a thousand. All during this time, the British government argued that nothing more could be done, despite pledges from the UN that Sarajevo was a 'safe area' and from Nato that it would prevent the 'strangulation' of the city. If air strikes were threatened or carried out, it was argued, the effect on the aid programme would be catastrophic and the risk to foreign troops, including British ones, would be unacceptable.

When I came back from Sarajevo I went to see a British official, who must remain unnamed because of the off-the-record nature of the meeting. He declared himself against air strikes, and sat back with his feet on the coffee-table scoffing at the people of Bosnia, whom he described airily as 'all pretty awful'. I recalled to myself, though not to him, the morning in Sarajevo when a string quartet gave a concert in an upstairs room overlooking the main street, very close to the central market. Anxious to try to convey some normality in a world gone mad, they had put on their dinner-jackets. They were playing a quartet by Grieg when a series of explosions erupted not far away. They missed not a note. They exchanged no glances of concern. Nor did the fifty people in the room, wrapped in overcoats against the cold, shift uneasily. No one moved: I was the only one who looked anxiously around. Afterwards the quartet's leader, a professor of music at the Conservatoire, remarked that bombs should not be allowed to gain victory over music. Was that man, I wondered, 'pretty awful'?

I felt then that British officials did not really know what was going on in Sarajevo. Britain, unlike France and the USA, has no ambassador there. Why not, I asked? 'We do not think it appropriate' was the reply. At that stage the Foreign Office was trotting out a line that the bombardment of Sarajevo was really the fault of the Bosnian government and army. They had 'provoked' the Serbs, it was argued, by firing into what Mr Hurd quaintly called 'that part of the city which is lived in by Serbs'. That part of the city is in fact an 'ethnically cleansed' area in central Sarajevo from which all but Serbs have been ejected. The Bosnian army had indeed attracted a savage response, some of which spilled over around the Holiday Inn where I was staying. But to take that isolated example as the pattern of behaviour seemed to me to represent a wrong-headed analysis of what was going on. If the British government thought that the Serbs were only bombarding Sarajevo in 'retaliation', no wonder it did not think it necessary to intervene. In fact the bomb last Saturday did not change the tactical and strategic balance in Sarajevo – yet policy did change. The impact of a single grave incident, reported in horrible detail on television and radio, galvanized Western governments. Suddenly, the arguments against intervention became less important: what mattered was to stop the shelling. Finally, the government saw the issue as most journalists had been describing it for months, and Mr Hurd became headmaster of the 'something-must-be-done' school.

ULTIMATUM FROM NATO

ALLAN LITTLE BOSNIA 19 FEBRUARY 1994

When the guns around Sarajevo were pulled back at the end of the winter, it was widely believed that the threat of air strikes from the West had caused the withdrawal of the Bosnian Serb artillery.

To begin with, it looked like another of those sleights of hand that we have come to recognize here. For a year and a half, UNPROFOR (the UN Protection Force) have not employed the threat of force that they have at their disposal. This has so debilitated them that it has involved them in successive public relations campaigns, the purpose of which has been to present failure as success, setback as breakthrough and humiliation at the hands of the Serbs as signs of support and cooperation. When, ten days ago, the UN commander here, General Rose, called a meeting between the Serbs and the Bosnian government at Sarajevo airport to try to agree on a weapons withdrawal programme on the same day that Nato was meeting in Brussels to decide the terms of its air strikes ultimatum, we thought it was the latest in a long and dishonourable tradition of UN practice here. We saw in it an attempt by UNPROFOR to pre-empt Nato's ultimatum and, therefore, detected a split in international opinion, a split between the UN and Nato, and a split between Nato countries, most notably Britain and the United States. Sceptics here declared that General Rose, a British general after all, from the country that has most consistently and most vigorously resisted the use of force, was charged with the mission of avoiding air strikes at whatever cost.

The sceptics, it seems, were wrong. But today's weapons withdrawal should be set in the context of what has passed these past twenty-two months. UNPROFOR, for me, reached the nadir of its impotence under its, to date, most flamboyant and ambitious general, Philippe Morillon. It occurred last April, when the Muslim enclave of Srebrenica was the focus of Serb territorial ambition. Every day, the advancing army was closing in. The Muslims were running out of ammunition, and were broadcasting desperate appeals for help from outside. The voice of the radio-ham operator – measured, calm but frightened and hideously alone and inaccessible – was that of a trapped animal waiting for its predator to approach.

General Morillon went into negotiations with the Serb general, Ratko Mladić, and asked for permission to send 120 Canadian troops to Srebrenica. General Mladić refused: his military task in the east was not yet finished, and he did not want international troops getting in the way. Lord Owen and Cyrus Vance intervened. General Mladić was called to Belgrade for further talks; at the end of that meeting an UNPROFOR spokeswoman told the press that a breakthrough had been achieved and that General Mladić supported and would co-operate with UNPROFOR's plan to station Canadians in Srebrenica. When General Mladić emerged, however, he said bluntly that the Canadians would go to Srebrenica 'over my dead body and those of my family'.

In the end the Canadians did go, but only after the military leaders in Srebrenica had begged the UN to move in and negotiate not a ceasefire but a surrender. Only then did General Mladić agree. This turn of events was interesting for two reasons. In Washington, the secretary of state had again asked the world to consider lifting the arms embargo against the Bosnians; in eastern Bosnia, the UN was moving in to *dis*arm them, in accordance with the surrender agreement written in large measure by the Serbs. And the focus of diplomatic pressure was on the Serbs to accept the then Vance–Owen plan, which restored Bosnian, not Serb, sovereignty to that part of eastern Bosnia. On the ground, again, the UN was doing the opposite, freezing the siege lines around the now tiny enclave.

The fighting stopped, but the Serbs had control. Something similar is happening here in Sarajevo this week, but there are crucial differences. There is a powerful anti-air strikes culture in UNPROFOR. They, after all, are the people on the ground who will suffer the retaliation such action could provoke. General Rose has inherited that mantle, and he too passionately wants to avoid air strikes. The difference now is that this stance will no longer be maintained at any cost, and the UN will not be allowed to present failure as success, setback as breakthrough, because this time Nato is watching and verifying from the air.

And, for the first time in Bosnia, the UN is no longer the sole arbiter of its own success or failure. For all their bluster and posturing, for all their cruelty, for all the atrocities they have committed, often gratuitously and to no apparent military effect, the Serb leaders have never been anything but rational in the military choices they have made. They know when they can win and when they can't. A credible threat of force from the West, aimed at clearly defined military and political objectives, appears to have worked.

There is a cemetery up the road from here that used to be a football field, and some of the 10,000 who have been killed in this city are buried there. Every time I go there, I wonder how many of them I have interviewed in the past few months. We are surely entitled to ask why that credible threat of force was not marshalled on the side of justice before now. More importantly, because the dead are gone, we are entitled to ask how it can be used, now that it has been so palpably successful, to prevent further injustice in the future. The 'something must be done' lobby appears to have had a point after all.

AS SEEN ON TV

KEVIN CONNOLLY   MOSCOW
26 FEBRUARY 1994

The transformation of Russia's economy, after the demise of the Soviet Union, has proved a traumatic business. But, little by little, the superficial signs of an emerging market economy have started to appear with luxury cars on the streets and new office buildings under construction. And now the very latest economic status symbol has arrived – satellite television.

Even more than the extension of the right to enter the Eurovision Song Contest, to countries not otherwise regarded as part of Europe, it is a rite of passage for the modern emerging market economy. At the end of a satellite television home-shopping programme, a screenful of national flags is flashed up with instructions to buy whatever you have just been watching. A few years ago there were just a few familiar banners from France, Germany, Great Britain, Sweden and the like, but these days the screen is a riot of colour, testament to the number of new states which have taken their rightful place among the nations of the world. I have friends in Slovenia and Lithuania who greeted the acquisition of the other trappings of statehood, like membership of the United Nations, with indifference, but who swear they had tears in their eyes when they first made it onto the screen. When your flag appears, together with a local telephone number and the price in your national currency, you can, I think, reasonably count yourself a citizen of the free world, with all the benefits that implies.

Those benefits, I can tell you from detailed first-hand study, include access to Willie Nelson compilation albums unavailable in the shops, a set of steak-knives guaranteed never to go blunt, and a small cooker shaped like a pork-pie hat which bakes a loaf of bread in fifteen minutes. The home-shopping services, it must be said, offer only the dimmest of windows on to the rest of the world. Their stock-in-trade is the half-hour programme about a particular product, punctuated by a two-minute commercial break in which you see a commercial about the same product, made out of material you have already seen earlier in the show. What you get, in other words, is the rhythm of ordinary television without the content.

It is not that the programmes are without entertainment value – my personal favourite is the one about the set of knives – but in form and content they all follow the same basic pattern. They start off with someone having a problem caused by the fact that they do not own the product being advertised. In this particular case it is a chef who picks up a knife with a great theatrical flourish and then finds it is too blunt to pierce a tomato. In fact, not only is it too blunt to pierce the tomato, it is so blunt the tomato keeps rolling away when he tries to cut it. (I know, it happens all the time.) The chef then turns to the camera and delivers the look of bewildered frustration which is the authentic hallmark of this whole televisual genre. Delivered by better actors it might convey the impotent sense of rage at the breakdown of daily life, which is its purpose. The programme then gets to the point, and stays there; this is where you really get sold something. The basic pitch is always towards saving time and money. 'After all,' runs the underlying message, 'get yourself stuck with a blunt vegetable knife and you could waste the whole weekend peeling that pile of potatoes.'

I personally find the idea of so much time being saved faintly depressing, if only because it implies that everyone else has always got something much more interesting to do than whatever it is they are currently doing. This is a world where hour-long chores are endlessly being reduced to ten-minute tasks and where hours are being saved every day. It is strange that, when of course the target audience already has so much time to kill, it is watching the home-shopping channel. But I suppose the producers would argue that they only have the time to watch it because they have already invested wisely in the sort of products advertised.

The money-saving pitch is just as unpersuasive. In this particular programme the chef, still labouring along with that tiny, rubber-bladed old knife that the rest of us use, produces – out of a potato the size of a small family car – a tiny scrap of cookable vegetable. Once again we are treated to a close-up look of rage and frustration, but we feel sorry for the actor too. This is not what you lie in bed and dream about on the night before your first day at drama school. There follows of course the offer, delivered by an unseen presenter speaking in a tone of rising astonishment, which makes you think that he is worried that the company will be forced out of business by its own reckless generosity. For the seasoned viewer there is always something faintly puzzling about the offer itself too. In this case, for example, you are given – yes, given – a multi-purpose knife which, it is suggested, is good for everything from trimming your nails to fashioning ocean-going balsa rafts. It is one of a set of thirty-three. But hold on a second, if this knife really does do everything, what are the other thirty-two for?

The programme closes, of course, with the same chef displaying a dazzling look of fulfilment. His knives are so good now that the vegetables in his kitchen peel themselves in the cupboard when they hear him opening the cutlery drawer. He is happy. On the home-shopping channel the only problem in anyone's life is the one directly related to non-ownership of whatever is currently being offered for sale.

Russia's flag is not up there on the screen just yet, but the pro-grammes, with their innocent acquisitiveness, are already wildly popular here. If that knife ever makes a visit to Moscow, it could find itself getting mobbed at the airport. This country has passed many milestones on the road to international economic integration in the last few years. When that flag finally appears on the screen, it will know it has truly acquired a market economy, and everything that goes with it.

GRUMPY RETURNS TO EURODISNEY

STEPHEN JESSEL   PARIS   26 FEBRUARY 1994

*The early days of the Eurodisney theme park near Paris were
punctuated by reports that there were acute financial difficulties,
that Europeans didn't want their own Disneyland and that the
weather was unsuitable anyway. We asked the BBC Paris Correspondent to return to Eurodisney to investigate.*

From the headquarters of a celebrated firm of accountants in Paris a
senior staff member set out earlier this week to deliver nine thick,
black files; one for each of the nine banks charged by some fifty-five
others with negotiating the future of Eurodisney. In each file was a
hundred-page report into the finances of the park which, when it last
reported its results, was losing money at the rate of £5 million a
week. Within the next five weeks the banks, owed over £2 billion,
and the Walt Disney company have to come to an agreement on
refinancing, the Disney people in the United States having promised
only to keep the park going until 31 March. Negotiations should be
brutal. The financial structure of the interlocking companies and
operators is of a complexity to baffle all but the experts. The banks
and the French government are desperate to save the park, their
investment and the related jobs. Disney will escape relatively lightly
in financial terms in the unthinkable event of the park closing, but
the blow to its prestige and image would be severe.

So one question is whether this vast project, with its gorgeous
palaces and cloud-capped towers out east of Marne la Vallée, can
survive; a second is whether it should. When the park opened twenty-
two months ago I reported on the event for *From Our Own Correspondent* in somewhat equivocal terms. Indeed, the editor saw fit to

include my report in the 1992 book of the programme under the title
'Grumpy Goes to Eurodisney' (rather perplexingly in my view, as
Grumpy is a figure from the Snow White legend, short, fat, bearded
and evil tempered).

I have been back; so many times, indeed, that I have lost count.
Things, it seems to me, have changed, although there is one further
obvious step to be taken: anyone holding or suspected of holding an
Italian passport should be required to take and pass an eight-hour
examination in the theory and practice of orderly queueing. Much of
what people know about the park is in fact false. The idea that it's
a chunk of the United States slapped down in Seine et Marne is not
really accurate. It is true that parts of it refer to an idealized vision
of small-town America at the turn of the century, but the park seems
to me to bear no resemblance at all to the contemporary reality. The
only guns are in the rifle range, the place is drug-free, you hardly
ever see a lawyer and almost nobody boasts about their wealth and
status. Nor is it the case that Disney characters dominate. You do see
Mickey and his pals around the place but anyone over the age of
about five is going to make for such rides as the admirable Star
Tours, the two roller-coasters, the haunted house or the Pirates of
the Caribbean – or, heaven help us, in the case of the strong-
stomached, the 3D Michael Jackson film. I hesitate to mention the
most developed example of kitsch in the known universe, the Small
World Ride, with its hundreds of grinning dolls in national costume
whirling to a treacly, but alas unforgettable, song.

Entry fees may not be low but once inside you do have the run
of the place for up to fifteen hours, and there are some good off-peak
deals. Nor are the park's problems caused primarily by a lack of
visitors. Targets have been more or less met, and even a Saturday in
February outside the school holidays brought a better than respectable
turnout. The problems are related more to a reluctance to buy food
and souvenirs and to stay in the hotels. Part of the hostility that
accompanied the early days of Eurodisney was the consequence of a
certain perceived arrogance and inflexibility on the part of the then
management. The view seemed to be that Disney was doing Europe
an enormous favour by consenting to bring its legendary expertise to
the old continent, and when you timidly asked about the suitability
of the site, pricing policies, the absence of alcohol and cultural differences, the questions were expertly deflected.

Since then the management has changed and the park has acquired a softer, gentler character. Prices have been substantially cut at some hotels and inside the park. Wine and beer are now available; actually this is more of a symbolic change because they are served only in four places, and only with meals, and in any case, there has always been a bar five minutes' walk away outside the main gate. But at least it was evidence of readiness to adapt to local conditions. In other ways, too, the place has become slightly Gallicized. Nobody ever thought that the 'have a nice day' paste-on smile of staff – sorry, cast members – in the American parks would transfer easily across the Atlantic (least of all to France) and it hasn't. But Europeans are more reserved than Americans, so why should an artificial chumminess be expected?

In a rather French way, it is apparent that some of the rules both for staff and for visitors are not always being enforced. Facial hair may be banned, but some male staff don't appear to shave on a daily basis. The technology, though breath-taking at its best, has a certain pleasing fallibility. Not one of my recent visits has been totally hitch-free, though none of the problems has been serious. All these things, I find, add to the park's charm by giving it a more human dimension. There's a strong case to be made that Marne la Vallée was the wrong choice and that Barcelona or another Spanish site would have been a better bet. And there's no doubting that the timing of the opening was wrong, coming as it did just as Europe was entering recession and several European currencies were devalued. Still, I've been to the park in rain and shine with companions ranging from small children to a distinguished academic of mature years, and they all loved it. Even Grumpy has been known to transmute, for the day anyway, into Happy.

WRESTLERS FOR HIRE

JULIAN BORGER   SOFIA   17 MARCH 1994

The wrestlers who once won gold medals for Bulgaria now find that they are no longer the state's favourites; they are having to look elsewhere for employment.

Say what you will about Bulgarian communism, but there were two things it could produce in glorious abundance: wrestlers and secret policemen. The regime mass-produced them – the wrestlers went out into the sporting arenas of the world and covered the country in glory and medals, while the spies, of course, went along with them to make sure they did not defect. It was a miracle of central planning. It may seem like an absurd piece of journalistic hyperbole but it is actually true that in the old days almost every Bulgarian family knew someone who was either a police informer or who knocked people over and sat on them for a living – or both. Now, of course, the old regime has passed away but its creatures, like Frankenstein's monster, live on and they are causing Bulgaria's shaky young democracy an enormous headache. For the spies and wrestlers, those two pillars of the communist state, have joined forces to produce a crimewave from hell.

Picture the scene, just after the fall of communism. The imposition of UN sanctions on neighbouring Serbia did for organized crime in Bulgaria what prohibition achieved in 1920s Chicago. Gangs who cut their teeth smuggling heroin from Turkey into Western Europe grew fat running millions of gallons of petrol across the Serbian border. When it came to recruiting Olympic-class muscle, the mobs were spoilt for choice. The streets were full of unemployed men who were designed by the old regime to personify the heavy-set virility of socialist labour – and they were in a very bad mood. Few groups lost quite so much financial backing and prestige when the old regime fell in 1989. With chips on their ample shoulders, they poured out of the gyms and into the streets, exchanging leotards for leather jackets and pistols. The Bulgarian word for 'the wrestlers' (*bortsite*) has now become the slang term for gangsters.

At more or less the same time, huge numbers of secret policemen found themselves on the job market as the country's first non-communist government spring-cleaned the Interior Ministry in 1991. The head of the ministry's anti-mafia department, Colonel Feodor Vladimirov, finds he spends much of his time trying to outwit former colleagues. Having told me this he seemed to feel obliged to add something in their defence. 'Of course,' he said, 'their role in these gangs is normally only an advisory one.'

In theory, the perfectly balanced gang would have a mix of wrestlers and ex-spies, a sort of yin-yang cocktail of brain and brawn, but it does not always turn out that way. One particular group composed principally of wrestlers has been fighting a territorial battle with a rival faction, led by former Interior Ministry men, over the market for protecting casinos. The struggle came to a head in a recent shoot-out at a plush gambling den in central Sofia owned by a former senior policeman. 'It was like a scene from a gangster movie,' said one eyewitness, a UN employee who had gone looking for a bit of Balkan nightlife. 'People were panicking and running in all directions, while all these big men in tuxedos were pulling out machine-guns.' For the time being the police appear to be outclassed and out-muscled. The day after the casino incident, they invited the head of one of the factions involved for coffee at the Interior Ministry, where they promptly arrested him. However, a big crowd of his men appeared in the ministry courtyard and the terrified police found themselves trapped. Two high-ranking officers were then sent to negotiate a compromise with one of the gang bosses' associates, apparently unaware that a separate police squad had been dispatched to arrest the same man. The result was an exchange of fire between the different groups of policemen, which left two dead and the suspect at liberty.

Organized crime has taken such a hold over the economy that it has overtaken privatization and land reform as the hottest political topic in parliament. The government of Prime Minister Lyuben Berov recently faced a vote of no confidence on the grounds that it had been unable to keep the gangs under control. Mr Berov survived, if only because most parliamentary deputies took a pessimistic view of their own chances of getting re-elected. President Zhelev, aware that he might soon be presiding over a thugocracy, was moved earlier this year to swallow previous moral objections and call for the temporary reintroduction of the death penalty, although he has admitted it was a concession to overwhelming public opinion and was unlikely to be effective. Meanwhile, the wrestling classes at Sofia's celebrated sports academy are reported to be as popular as ever, echoing with the thud of bull-necked young Bulgarians hitting rubber mats. But these days all the pain and effort is no longer seen as a path to Olympic glory, but rather as an easy way to get an armlock on a secure career in one of Bulgaria's few growth industries.

BANDIT CITY

TIM SEBASTIAN   ST PETERSBURG
14 APRIL 1994

The explosion in crime in Russia that followed the end of communist rule is proving to be a nightmare for police and public alike. Crime now permeates all sections of society and ranges from mugging, robbery and theft through rape and murder to large-scale mafia activity and multi-million-dollar swindles. And the police are unable to do much about it.

Colonel Orlov and I were not having a good evening. It was 3 a.m. on a Friday night in the miserable, run-down police station on Chekhov Street, right in the city centre. The place had not been painted or repaired in forty years. Below us the station sergeant was listening to 1930s dance music on a tinny little loudspeaker. If it were not for the shocking crime rate, you would have thought we were lost without trace in the 1950s. To make us both tea, Orlov inserted an electric element into a jam-jar of water. He spread a piece of newspaper on the desk and cut a loaf of bread into slices. 'Let's have supper,' he said. It was a chance for Orlov to give vent to some of the growing frustrations about a police force that is bought and corrupted by organized crime, that has not got enough cars to get to the raids it plans and that leaks information like a paper bag in a storm.

'You have to be an enthusiast to work here,' he said. 'I dream of a time when we'll have computers connected to something, when I don't have to spend half the day on the phone trying to find out the owner of a car. Things like that.' He grinned and cut another slice of bread. His boss came in. 'You want to see how we work? Look at this,' he said, and picked up the phone. 'Try getting the emergency service.' We dialled 02. 'See,' he said gleefully, 'it's engaged.' We tried again. This time it was answered after a minute and a half. He laughed out loud. 'You don't want to be in trouble in this city. Even under the best circumstances, the very best, we couldn't react in under twenty minutes. Maybe half an hour. What use is that?'

Around four in the morning, a young man was bought into Orlov's office in handcuffs and sat on the bench beside the rickety old desk. He was suspected of stealing a woman's fur coat, no trivial crime in these sub-zero temperatures. 'I didn't take it,' he said, 'but I know where it is.' Orlov looked up wearily. 'Let me go and I'll bring it back to you.' Orlov nodded and leaned back in his chair. 'Where are you living?' he asked. The man named a hotel near one of the railway stations. 'How come you're living there? Are you registered?' 'I'm not registered,' said the man. And then there was a little flash of pride. 'I'm a businessman. You know how it is?' A businessman? I am old enough to remember the time when every second person you met in Russia was an artist, a *khudozhnik*. Well, this businessman was heading for a minor slap on the wrist, and then he would be out again, selling his wares, or someone elses's wares. Bought, stolen – as one of the city's leading crooks said to me: 'We don't make money here in Russia, we steal it.'

Faced with a new breed of criminal entrepreneur, Orlov and his colleagues are not just outclassed, they are not even in the race. They do not solve crimes, they register them, if they are lucky. According to the city's police chief their business these days is to provide the remnants of social order for the tired and tortured people of St Petersburg. And when he says remnants, he means it. The murder rate, even according to official figures, is around nine hundred a year, considerably higher than for the whole of Britain. In fact, the real figures may be twice as high. I am told that the officials have begun, once again, to massage the statistics.

At least 90 per cent of the city's businesses maintain direct contacts with the Russian mafia, the thirty or forty families who control the city's trade from the smallest kiosk to the largest factory. I'm not talking about criminal contacts, but about criminal control, absolute and total – the emergence of the world's first superpower gangster state. And if you think that is an exaggeration, then go out and talk to the people who have had their kiosks burned to the ground, their livelihoods destroyed, their businesses trampled on and robbed by crooks. Arthur is one of those gangsters. He belongs to a group that has been on a killing spree for several months now, culling the ranks of the opposition. When they are not 'working' – extortion, racketeering, and so on – he and his colleagues congregate in the coffee-bars of the major new hotels. I will not describe Arthur, because that would not be clever. But he has a tough handshake and a new interest in international business.

'We have many contacts now in Germany and America,' he said, laying his portable phone down on the table. The BMW was parked outside, the jacket was quality leather. I could not help drawing a contrast between him and the police from the station on Chekhov Street. Arthur also professes himself to be a businessman. 'I can get round all the regulations,' he said. 'I know how to do it without paying any tax at all. Not a penny.' This is the world according to Arthur – and increasingly it is being run his way. The crooks have filled the vacuum created by state confusion and incompetence, and a level of corruption scarcely imaginable in a giant modern state. Russia is not about justice. It is about which hand is stronger, which gun has more bullets in it, who can shoot straighter, who can pay the larger bribes.

'Don't ever forget who you're dealing with,' said an underworld contact. 'Violent, ruthless people, many times more savage than your own criminals in the West. They're born out of economic hardship,' he told me. 'We have a saying in Russia: "the hungry wolf runs faster".' Well, these hungry wolves have not just run faster, they have run off. And what is more, they have dragged the country with them.

VIVE LA DIFFÉRENCE

STEPHEN JESSEL   PARIS   30 APRIL 1994

The opening to the general public of the Channel Tunnel may have been seriously delayed, but it did not prevent the Queen and the French president from taking part in a lavish opening ceremony. It came during a year full of Franco-British events that spotlighted the ties between the two nations, but also the old antagonism that exists between them.

It is a handsomely produced document, on high-quality paper, with many pictures, thirty-two pages in all, and it will be printed and distributed on both sides of the Channel in its thousands. It is a brochure, and it seeks to sell not time-share holidays or financial services but something infinitely more elusive: Franco-British understanding. It aims, says a foreword, to illustrate the solid nature of the relationship between the two sides and it sets out to do so by detailing the commercial, cultural, scientific, diplomatic and other links between the two countries.

The timing of this unique exercise, in which each government tries to persuade its citizens of the value of their relationship with a close neighbour, arises from the coincidence of three major Franco-British events. One, of course, is the official opening of the Channel Tunnel, although I permit myself to say that some of us went through it more than four months ago. The tunnel, even if it is still some way from being fully operational, does constitute a physical link between Britain and France for the first time for some thousands of years as well as being the product of close financial and technical cooperation. The second happening is the commemoration of the fiftieth anniversary of the D-day landings on the beaches of lower Normandy, the start of the liberation of France by an allied force of which British troops were a substantial element. And the third event is the ninetieth anniversary of the Entente Cordiale, signed in 1904, amid some grumbling in France, to end the rivalries in the scramble for African colonies and to inaugurate a new era of cooperation and friendship, with few foreseeing that this new partnership would be put to the practical test ten years later in the killing fields of Picardy and Flanders.

Three Franco-British events within the space of nine weeks provide reason enough for the authors of the brochure to talk of the entente cordiale of today and to remind people that two very different nations have more in common than it sometimes seems. They have more or less identical populations and long imperial histories, they are middle-ranking players on the world stage, possessors of nuclear weapons, cultural powers and members – for the time being anyway – of the United Nations Security Council. These days they even have an increasingly similar attitude to the European Union, with a substantial section of the French governing coalition holding views about its future that would by no means displease the Euro-sceptic wing of the Conservative Party. We have not even fought each other for the last 179 years. On both sides of the Channel there are people who realize this community of interest, without being blind to the real conflicts that do exist in some areas. But the very fact of the publication of the brochure, admirable in many ways as it is, shows how little this is generally recognized in the two countries and prompts the thought that a more effective use of the money might have been to pay Eric Cantona of Manchester United to tour Britain as a goodwill ambassador for his country.

One of the less agreeable duties of a British correspondent in France is to be interviewed periodically by the French media, which are genuinely puzzled by the need of some of their British counterparts to be so foully offensive about France and the French. The tabloids, stuck in their sad war-comic world of Frogs and Huns, they half understand; but when what used to be known as the quality press starts to sing the same song, they do become perplexed. British friends with whom I discuss this tend to say: 'Ah yes, but the French are just as rude about us.' That is not, in my experience, true; they do call us *rosbifs* occasionally and you can find embittered people who can reel off perfidies from Joan of Arc to stolen jobs via Fashoda and Mers el Kebir and franglais, but they are a very small minority, and the much larger number who are critical of the British policy and what they see as a slavish subservience to the United States manage generally to voice their objections without reference to personal cleanliness, physical cowardice, eating habits and the rest of the dreary canon of schoolboy insults. My reply to my French questioners is that anti-French sentiment is in fact a more generalized xenophobia directed at France only because for the Briton, or more precisely for the Englishman, the Frenchman is by virtue of history and physical nearness the foreigner *par excellence*. The French, by contrast, have a rich array of neighbours to vilify if the mood so takes them, eight contiguous states or statelets; Britain, across a stretch of water, makes nine and the sheer number of neighbours may, incidentally, explain why the tunnel excites the French less than it does the British. What is one more land frontier among so many?

The brochure may change attitudes, though I rather doubt it. British officials anxious to deflect suspicions that the aim of current policy is less to reinforce Franco-British ties than to woo Paris away from Bonn insist that the initiative is not directed against anyone. This is a wise move since, for the French, the Germans will always be the privileged partners of choice while London will always look longingly across the Atlantic, and where misunderstandings can take place they will continue to do so. A French academic recently published a very funny satire on the learning of English. It was interpreted by the British press, of course, but also by part of the French press, as a brutal and underhand attack on Britain. The poor man is in despair. It was the French he was trying to lampoon.

TALL STORIES

KEVIN CONNOLLY   MOSCOW   30 APRIL 1994

*Russian newspaper stories often seem far-fetched, even incredible.
Nevertheless, they may be telling the reader a great deal about the
country and the way its people live.*

It is midnight as the coach approaches the Russian frontier on the
way to Poland, and a group of tourists is propping up the body of a
fellow holiday-maker who has died of a heart attack and putting
sunglasses on him so that customs officers will not realize he is dead
and hold up the holiday. In the silence of a pensioner's apartment in
a small provincial town a conscience-stricken burglar is working out
how much it will cost to repair the front door he has broken down
and leaving the money with a covering note. After an epidemic of
petty pilfering, the staff of a state-run restaurant drill holes in all the
soup-spoons in order to make them so annoying to use that no one
will want to steal them.

These visions of life in modern Russia are gleaned from a variety
of local newspapers which, in recent weeks, have also brought news
of the man who built an Olympic swimming-pool on the ninth floor
of a block of flats and of the Yeti-style creature with a special tail
that rubs out the huge footprints it would otherwise be leaving in the
snow as proof of its existence. There were also the stories of the town
that offered a bottle of vodka to anyone who could prove they had
shot a stray dog, and the crew of the fire-engine who turned up at a
blazing block of flats so drunk that they managed to set their own
vehicle alight. The papers are telling tales of violence, cruelty, ec-
centricity, wealth and incompetence and, of course, they are almost
all, almost certainly, made up.

Every so often it is the job of the foreign journalist to follow up
such stories, to find the fire crew, interview the tourists, inspect the

soup-spoons at first hand and so on. This can be a time-consuming task in a country that does not have telephone directories to help you track people down and is still using telephone exchanges looted from the ruins of Nazi Germany at the end of the war. The starting point is usually the journalist who wrote the story in the first place; usually he or she is the finishing point as well. It does not normally take more than a few minutes to establish that there is little or no substance to most of the stories.

It is not, of course, that the stories of modern life here are invented. They have invariably happened to a friend of the writer, to a member of his family or, in one case, to the friend of a man the journalist overheard talking in a bus queue. It must be a nerve-racking business being the friend of anyone who writes for a local newspaper here. The stories are, as the author of one such report patiently explained to me, true, but in a general rather than a specific sense. It is, she argued, frustrating to know that you live in the kind of country where such things happen and not to be able to illustrate them because you do not happen to have the right kind of examples to hand.

Local newspapers in Russia are certainly learning to enjoy their new freedom. Liberation from the need to provide detailed coverage of the doings of the local Communist Party establishment must, after all, be a heady experience. But this turmoil in the world of Russian journalism is reflected on the national stage too. Publications like *Pravda*, *Literaturnaya Gazeta* and *Trud* used to be among the best-selling in the world even though, with their crowded pages of tiny type and smudgy black-and-white passport-sized photos, they looked like wartime knitting patterns.

They were paid for by subcription and, in the era of fixed prices and state subsidies, cost almost nothing. They must have been piling up unread in flats all over Russia but commercially they did not have a care in the world. In the cold world of the free market, things are rather different. The price of newsprint, ink, labour, electricity, of almost everything, has multiplied a thousand times. Few titles are distributed outside a handful of the main cities, and even there they are often late.

The coverage of politics, sport, economics and culture has improved, of course, but the new Russia is discovering the staples of tabloid journalism, sex, stardom and scandal, and the newspapers are not bringing the people what they want. Why else would a magazine that started life as an AIDS information sheet and rapidly converted itself into a guide to sex now apparently have sales of more than five million? This is a publication that once carried a personal ad saying simply: 'Man wants sex.'

If you are an optimist, of course, you believe that this is a period of licence inevitable after decades of repression and that sober, responsible journalism will develop and fill what is, at the moment, a gap in the market. Perhaps it will. But for the moment, it is worth reflecting, as a local newspaper editor once told me, that even when the stories you read in Russia are not true they could be telling a great deal about life here as the people who live here see it.

REFUGEES IN LIMBO

WILLIAM HORSLEY   BERLIN   5 MAY 1994

Bloody conflicts such as those in Bosnia and Rwanda swelled the number of people seeking asylum in Germany to more than two million. But after the spate of violent attacks against refugee homes in the country, the German authorities started deporting people faster than new asylum-seekers could arrive. It meant that numerous people were living in fear of deportation while others went underground to try to avoid capture.

Nseka Ousman is in hiding – in Germany or France, or somewhere else in Europe. Three weeks ago I met him in Berlin. His intelligent face wore a hunted look. He is thirty years old, and after five years living in limbo in Germany as an asylum-seeker from Zaire, his last appeal to stay had been turned down. He expected the police to come for him at any time. It was an imminent threat, as 37,000 asylum-seekers were deported from Germany last year, many after several years in refugee homes, and the pace of the forced exodus has quickened this year. The deportees went back to various countries in Africa, to Romania, to Bulgaria and some to former Yugoslavia. Detailed facts are hard to come by, although it is known that thousands have been sent away through a sealed-off part of Berlin's Schönefeld Airport.

Nseka told me that he had been a dissident student and a member of the political opposition to the government of President Mobutu in Zaire. If he were sent back, he said, he would be suspected at once because of his bid to gain asylum abroad. At the airport in Zaire, he said, the police would take all his belongings, and they could throw him in jail. Nobody would know. He might even be killed. It was a story of dismaying familiarity among the would-be refugees who have crowded into Germany as their gateway to the West. Nseka added that, for him, life in Berlin was bad. He was barred from steady work, and even though he spoke German, he had grown used to being insulted because of his skin colour and to hearing the words 'Foreigners, go home!'

Nseka showed me the thick sheaf of official papers about his case. On the front was the key sentence, dated March 1991: 'The application for the right to receive asylum is refused.' Inside were the justifications for the decision: a statement, also three years old, that multi-party democracy was coming to Zaire and an allegation, made one year ago, that his wish for asylum was merely an attempt to evade his quite legitimate deportation. I was in no position to judge the particulars of Nseka's case, but Amnesty International told me that persecution and police brutality were now so commonplace in Zaire that no one should be deported there. The UN Refugee Agency agreed that Amnesty's assessment held true for people from certain regions of Zaire, but said that it had not yet recommended a total ban on deportations there.

Shortly afterwards Nseka was taken into detention, but friends from his refugee home and Christian action groups managed to get him released after one day. Since then, probably with their help, he has disappeared. He has joined a small army of would-be refugees, many thousands strong, refused an extension of stay in Germany or a nearby country, without hope of recognition anywhere in Europe, hiding, praying, living illegally, some seeking sanctuary in churches and all hoping against hope that they won't be captured. Germany is faced with a refugee crisis of monumental proportions. It is putting grave strains on the nation's finances, its police, its administration and courts and on its traditional post-war political liberalism too. The figures are staggering. Including the nearly 200,000 people who have won legal asylum in Germany, almost one in every fifty people in the country today is or would like to be called a refugee. Four hundred thousand of them have fled from civil wars. Germany's liberal laws allowed these people in, but despite protests from international refugee agencies, the law also excludes them from gaining the formal status of refugees, and the security that could bring. Sooner or later they are to be sent away. Three-quarters of a million people are officially in limbo after being told that they cannot stay, and about half a million more are still going through Germany's complex asylum procedure. After last year's tightening of the rules the prospect for many is that, after the statutory two court hearings, they too will join the stream of deportees. Germany's laws now mean that anyone found entering Germany without permission from Poland or the Czech Republic to the east, or indeed from any other direction, is returned over the border when caught. Further lists of so-called safe countries, in eastern Europe and parts of Africa, have made the conscience-troubling business of mass deportations easier. But to ask the individuals involved about their fate is to look into the soul of a Europe that has grown hard-hearted. The bare facts are there for all to see. In Germany alone there are two million people in a kind of purgatory, waiting for the knock on the door or the official note to say their time is up. And last year alone there were 248 fire-bomb attacks on refugee homes by young Germans who believe blindly in the slogan that has made Nseka from Zaire a bitter man: 'Foreigners go home!'

THE MIDDLE EAST

THE HANDSHAKE THAT MADE HISTORY

ALEX BRODIE   JERUSALEM   18 SEPTEMBER 1993

In signing their historic accord in Washington the Palestine Liberation Organization and the Israeli government achieved something many thought to be impossible. Even more extraordinary was the fact that the man who shook the hand of PLO Chairman Yasser Arafat was Israeli Prime Minister Yitzhak Rabin, a man who had spent his life fighting wars against Israel's Arab neighbours and who, as defence minister, had come down hard on Palestinian insurgents.

Yasser Arafat beaming, Yitzhak Rabin venturing only a wry grin, the two shook hands before the eyes of the world. Behind them was Bill Clinton, arms wide as if to encompass them both and urge them together. This was the picture that went around the world, the handshake of enemies. The spectacle was riveting for Israelis and Palestinians alike because of the pain, the history, the killing, the hatred, the passions. To many, and I believe to most, Palestinians it marked the end of a road that was petering out anyway in despair and bitterness and the start of new hope of life without the humiliation of occupation. As for the Israelis, the nation was holding its breath – a cliché, yes, but in this case an unavoidable one, for it was true. Whereas Palestinians in Gaza, Jericho and elsewhere spilled out onto the streets joyously to wave their flag, for once without fear of having it snatched from them at the point of a soldier's gun, Israelis stayed at home and watched.

They watched as their prime minister emerged from the White House beside the man they had learned, over a quarter of a century, to loathe. He appeared just as they had expected – stubbly beard, military-style uniform, black-and-white *keffiyeh* on his head. All that was missing was the gun at his hip. They watched to see how their prime minister would handle this encounter with the enemy: would he or wouldn't he shake his hand? When the moment came it was high drama. In Israel, one imagined, there would have been a collective gasp before hundreds of thousands of television sets. In the office building in Jerusalem where I was watching, a pin-drop silence was followed by the gasp and then a cheer.

It is impossible to overestimate the symbolic power of that handshake. The way Mr Rabin handled it did a lot for his chances of carrying his people with him, for he *was* them. He behaved as they probably would have done. He displayed the ambiguity about the encounter that they were feeling; he was ill at ease, awkward, wondering how much he had to do, what he could get away with not doing. He behaved as you do when standing next to someone you do not actually want to look at. He fidgeted and gazed around, anywhere but in Arafat's direction. When the moment came, he seemed to take a deep breath, turned, looked at him in the eye and did it, and when it was done, released a small smile of relief. He said he had butterflies in his stomach, he said it was not easy. He spoke directly to, and shared the apprehensions of, Middle Israel.

Thus the way he behaved and spoke was politically astute, and got him off to a flying start in his campaign to take the country with him. Mr Rabin also has the great advantage of being deemed sound on security – it is one big reason why he won the last election. He embraces the highly popular, among Israelis, doctrine of overwhelming responses. It was he who dispatched 400 alleged Islamic militants to exile in south Lebanon, to the horror of the world outside but to the delight of his people, who backed the draconian measure overwhelmingly. Moreover, this summer he ordered the bombardment of villages in southern Lebanon with the aim of creating a quarter of a million refugees in order to make a point to the government in Beirut. In persuading Israelis to trust the peace deal Mr Rabin's 'hard man' image is an asset. The deal must yield fruit soon, and change is planned to be swift. Military withdrawal from the Gaza Strip and Jericho is due to begin on 13 December and to be completed by April. During the same time in the rest of the West Bank, troops will be redeployed outside populated areas, and throughout the occupied territories, excluding Jerusalem, authority will be transferred to the Palestinians in the areas of education and culture, health, social welfare, direct taxation and tourism. Elections to a Palestinian Council to run self-rule are to be held not later than July.

However, decades of distrust and mutual contempt do not disappear overnight. Many Palestinians find it hard to believe that Israeli troops will withdraw from their lives. A Palestinian friend who has lived all his life under occupation and has been arrested, imprisoned and casually mistreated said he could not imagine living in freedom, nor did he believe he ever would. But that has not curbed the excitement and elation he is now feeling.

Many, probably most, Israeli Jews feel trepidation and caution. At the back of their minds lurks the Holocaust-inspired image of themselves as victims. Despite their many times victorious army, their nuclear arsenal, the support of the greatest power on earth and their stable parliamentary system, many Israelis remain insecure and afraid. Today what they fear particularly is Islamic militancy. It got the better of them in Lebanon, and they worry lest the Gaza Strip turn into another Lebanon. For many reasons the comparison is not yet valid, although the Islamic movement is strong in Gaza. However, its main recruiter has always been the Israeli occupation. While the mainstream PLO was being seen to be humiliated at the peace table and getting nowhere, the Islamic group Hamas offered angry young men pride, faith and combat. With realities about to change it is not clear just how deep Hamas's roots in Gaza are.

THE KING AND
MR ARAFAT

ALEX BRODIE   JERUSALEM   19 FEBRUARY 1994

As the Israelis and Palestinians edged closer to implementing their historic peace deal, the PLO leader Yasser Arafat was having regular meetings with King Hussein of Jordan. But how much distrust and rivalry lay behind the public embraces?

The Jordanians call it King Hussein Bridge, and the Israelis still call it the Allenby Bridge after the British general who took Jerusalem from the Turks in 1917. But most, on both sides, know it simply as 'The Bridge' – a narrow, rattling gangway of wooden planks across the River Jordan which, amid a biblical landscape of barren dunes, is disappointingly little more than a muddy stream. This hot, sleepy place, at just about the lowest point on earth, is potentially a Middle Eastern crossroads. It is where Israel meets a vast Arabia with which it is still officially at war. For Islam, it is a passageway, at present constricted, to its third holiest site just twenty miles up the hill in Jerusalem; for the nascent Palestinian state, or whatever it is to become, it is a doorway to the Arab world. For the bridge is only a couple of miles from Jericho, where Yasser Arafat plans to set up his headquarters.

It is important to all, and so after countless hours of haggling and brinkmanship, it has been decided that there will soon be three flags flying at the bridge: Israeli, Jordanian and Palestinian. That is a complex triangular relationship. Palestinians are Israeli, Jordanian and stateless. The other day, crossing on foot, I was able to linger at the precise centre, where the porter from the Israeli side dumped my bags to await the porter from Jordan. It was a good place to contemplate the conflict: between two sets of border guards, an Arab army on one bank, the Jewish army on the other. Above, facing each other across the Dead Sea, were the hills of Judea and Jordan – including Mount Nebo, where God is said to have shown Moses the promised land and from where today you can see on the skyline the tallest building in Jerusalem. It is, prosaically, the Holiday Inn.

We foreigners are privileged to be able to cross the bridge. Israelis cannot, at least not without concealing their true identity – the antithesis of the recognition they crave. Palestinians need special permission, and then they have to submit themselves to humiliating and lengthy searches and interrogation at the hands not just of Israelis but also of Jordanians. I had to go along with the fiction that I had not travelled from Israel, so as I stood in the middle of the bridge I was deemed to have just materialized there. One passport was discreetly put away and another, unsullied by any Israeli stamp, produced. This fiction reflects official absurdity but not reality.

King Hussein himself recently admitted that, throughout the forty-one years of his reign, he has met secretly every Israeli prime minister bar one, that one being Menachem Begin. There is unacknowledged but extensive security cooperation between the two enemies, usually in relation to the Palestinians, a time-bomb that both are holding and neither can quite defuse. Israel and Jordan have each occupied the West Bank and suppressed the Palestinians. In Black September 1970 King Hussein, fearing for his throne, went to war against the state within his state and threw out the PLO. Just as Israel cannot allow back within what are now its borders the refugees of the 1948 war, for fear of Jews being outnumbered by Arabs, so Jordan too is driven by fear of outnumbering. Palestinians may already constitute a majority, though the king and his courtiers do not like to admit it.

So King Hussein and Yasser Arafat are in direct competition for the hearts and minds of the Palestinians. Arafat's contest with the Israelis is relatively simple: it is over the land. His contest with the king is over the land and the people. I often work in the Palestinian refugee camps of the Israeli occupied territories, and frequently record the views of the inmates. They can, and do, say what they wish. I found it ironic that in a camp in Jordan I was followed and questioned by Jordanian security police and forbidden to talk to residents of the camp, who dare not speak their minds publicly. A 'vox pop' here was out of the question. The Israelis care what Palestinians under their control do. The Jordanians care what they do and say. Another fiction must be preserved: that of total loyalty to the king. Palestinian flags and pictures of Yasser Arafat are still not openly displayed in the refugee camps of Jordan. In the Israeli occupied territories, they are.

Under any conceivable peace deal, most of the 1.5 million or so Palestinians in Jordan will stay. Thus the king must ensure that they are Jordanians first and Palestinians second. He, and only he among Arab rulers, has given citizenship to the Palestinians he hosts. He does not want any more, and he needs to ensure that Jordan does not become a dumping-ground for 600,000 stateless refugees currently in Lebanon and Syria. What is at stake is nothing less than his kingdom. The fantasy of the Israeli right, that Jordan is Palestine, is his nightmare. For Jordan, peace is about solving the refugee problem and it is best done by Arabs together, by a comprehensive deal. King Hussein is thus affronted by Arafat's secret separate deal with Israel, which has produced another of those ironies – that the Israelis now build up their erstwhile foe, Yasser Arafat, while the Jordanians make it clear that they do not trust him an inch. It may well be mutual, for Yasser Arafat certainly has reason to be wary of the king who, without doubt, has ambitions to stage a comeback in the West Bank if Arafat messes it up or outlives his usefulness. By doing a deal with the PLO, Israel has set loose Palestinian nationalism, a beast of unsure direction. The game has only just begun.

LAST DAYS OF THE MARSH ARABS?

TIM LLEWELLYN   QRNA   24 FEBRUARY 1994

Since the end of the Gulf War, Saddam Hussein has restarted the huge drainage and irrigation programme begun more than thirty years ago. The Iraqi regime maintains that it is part of a plan to modernize the country, to provide water for cultivation and food, but critics say it is designed to destroy the age-old culture of the Marsh Arabs.

The Arab marshes, the Howeyza, cover an inaccessible region of about seven thousand square miles in south-eastern Iraq roughly between Amara in the north, Basra in the south, the Iranian border to the east and Nasariyeh and the Iraqi desert to the west. They shield a mystery, impenetrable and dangerous as they always have been. The Madan, the Marsh Arabs, could trace their unique, aboriginal way of life back more than three thousand years if they knew how to. It was a world of waterways, towering reeds, rich, exotic and nourishing bird life, fish to spear, deftly woven homes and *mudhifs* – tall, arched meeting places, perched gracefully on the water's edge.

The impenetrability of the marshes is the source of their troubles, their continuing metamorphosis and the often exaggerated and one-sided stories that leak out from time to time. Genocide is talked of, as are chemical weapons, the end of a civilization, brutality, repression, murder and terror, and a panicky exodus by these simple, historical people fleeing our favourite tyrant, Saddam Hussein. Stories of the horror in the Iraqi marshes come from the Iranian side of the border, where tens of thousands of people have fled to camps, from refugees under Iranian supervision and from Iraqi opposition groups housed and supported by Iran. Travel into the marshes from the east is

135

launched in a closely monitored setting, and is sufficiently dangerous that it has to be done by night, in extreme stealth. Not everything is what it seems. Smuggled film is readily taken by visiting sympathizers to show what the activists say it shows.

On the other side – my side, if you like, on this occasion – the Iraqis who accompanied me were no more forthcoming. Government officials took me down the long road south, across the endless sands, speeding past the date palms and shabby villages and lone, robed figures eking out God knows what sort of a living. In the busier marshes, my guides were joined by officials from the local Ba'ath Party. Any illusion of spontaneity was destroyed by the Iraqis themselves when a line of cheering children danced out of a village, carrying pictures of their leader and chanting slogans and speeches. I went where I was taken and saw what the Iraqis wished me to. In these circumstances, as I have found on two recent visits to the marshes, it is easy to describe what I see, harder to guess what is happening a few miles away.

'Is it a crime that we want to develop people, bring them out of the Dark Ages, improve their health and welfare and build up our own foodstocks?' a former Iraqi ambassador had asked me, in a slightly pained way, in Baghdad. Down here in Qrna, twenty miles from the Iranian frontier, it was certainly hard to deny him his view, on the available evidence. The great flat stretch of the man-made Saddam River runs 350 miles long and more than a mile wide, north-west to south-east, between the Tigris and the Euphrates. It is linked to canals, which cross the marshes. Its drainage, a sort of laundering process, takes the murderous salt off the lands so that wheat, barley and rice can be grown. I could see it happening: tomatoes were growing under plastic covers. It is working.

In a *mudhif*, an elegant meeting-house about forty feet long, fifteen feet high and ten feet wide, built in a Gothic arch from tightly woven reeds, able to withstand extreme heat, cold and rain, the Shi'ite Muslim saint Ali stared down, a revered martyr. Next to him, inevitably, was a portrait of Saddam Hussein. We grabbed fistfuls of rice and freshly slaughtered lamb, the animal's head on a plate by my side, a mark of respect for the honoured guest, staring ruefully at me. No-one was anything but upbeat about the new life of the marshes.

The villagers have been given substantial amounts of government money to move to the new canals, where they still have their reeds and water buffalo, but there are now brick houses, electricity, sanitation, clean drinking water, a clinic and farmland, as well as fishing, hunting and the supply of reeds for houses and for local factories making paper and cardboard. Life is changing for the better, it appears. Neither is this a new process – the drainage and re-irrigation of the Arab marshes was planned in the 1950s, and started in earnest in the 1970s. Gavin Young, a protégé of the explorer Wilfred Thesiger, wrote seventeen years ago about the modernization he had witnessed, worrying then that the Madan might suffer the same fate as the Amazonians in the rainforests. The projects were restarted in earnest nearly three years ago after the Gulf War, when labour was plentiful and a new food-base was badly needed amid the depredations of trade sanctions and an oil embargo that denies Iraq foreign currency and therefore the bulk of the imports on which it had depended. Iraq's own farming industry had long been neglected.

'The West just doesn't want us to progress,' grumbled an old villager, when I asked him about his changing way of life, the worries Gavin Young expressed nearly twenty years ago, and the ones that more politically motivated people have now. This resentment of the West crops up from time to time, encouraged by the Iraqi regime, no doubt, but perhaps understandable at a time of sanctions, inflation, unemployment and hopelessness. I thought then of the other human beings who have had to change in the name of progress: my forebears in the Welsh mines, or on the slopes of now-flooded valleys, the tin industry of Cornwall and the small farmer. We see such change as essential for us, but as an ominous development in the romantic fastnesses of the Orient. We object to seeing a Toyota Corolla where Freya Stark once rode a donkey. The controversy is electrified by the suspicion that, eco-systems and agriculture apart, Saddam Hussein is marooning and murdering an age-old people.

There is no doubt that bad things are happening in the marshes, but when it comes to genocide and mass slaughter the evidence so far is suspect, partisan. The marshes have always been the route for marauding Persian Khans, the hideaways for Iraq's enemies, outlaws and bandits. The Iranians came again and again between 1980 and 1988, nearly but never quite to Basra, Amara and Qrna. And then again, three years ago, the marshes were the passageway for invading Iranian and exiled Iraqi gunmen, in support of the rebellion against Saddam; they were their escape-route and their sanctuary when that revolt was crushed.

Saddam may be an international pariah and regional menace, but he can hardly be blamed for wanting to make the marshes safe, for him and for his nation's security. I think this is a side-benefit of, not the main reason for, the man-made rivers. Whoever supposes there is only one reason for anything?

HEBRON MASSACRE

ALEX BRODIE   JERUSALEM   3 MARCH 1994

When an Israeli fanatic pulled out a gun and shot dead twenty-nine Arabs as they prayed in Hebron, rioting broke out in the West Bank and Gaza Strip, more lives were lost and it was feared that the action might deal a fatal blow to the Israeli–Palestinian peace process. But it raised the difficult question of the Israeli settlers to the top of the agenda.

In the midst of the fury and bloody aftermath of a vile slaughter it is difficult, if not positively eccentric, to talk of peace. The massacre of Palestinians at prayer in Hebron has certainly done terrible, possibly terminal, damage to the particular peace plan under negotiation – but in the long run it just may have saved the peace. For the massacre has exposed the fatal flaw at the heart of the Gaza Jericho First Plan: the Jewish settlers. They are the fundamental contradiction of the peace process.

The ideological core of settlers believe that God gave the land to them: it is theirs, not the Arabs', and it is their mission permanently to conquer the occupied territories. The two million Arab inhabitants are an inconvenience. The settlements are there precisely to stop any 'land for peace' deal, which is what this peace process, at root, constitutes. Yet the process has been adapted and convoluted to accommodate the settlers – the very people who are dedicated to destroying it.

Under the Gaza Jericho First Plan, the settlements are to be left in place, Jewish enclaves amidst Palestinian self-government, with their ultimate fate to be decided only when the permanent status of the occupied territories is negotiated. I think it is the hope of the Israeli prime minister, Mr Rabin, that the settlements will wither on the vine, start to die a natural and uncontroversial death and not disrupt too badly the workings of Palestinian self-rule. That might work with settlements which stand alone in the hills, or are self-contained with wire around them, but it certainly cannot work with Hebron. The peace deal requires Israeli troops to withdraw from Arab towns but allows them to remain to protect Jewish settlements. In the case of Hebron, those two things are mutually exclusive because the settlement is in the city. Nor is Hebron a problem susceptible to woolly liberal solutions along the lines of 'everything will be all right if two peoples can just be persuaded to coexist peacefully'. Coexistence is impossible: the Jews and Arabs in Hebron loathe each other and want to see each other dead. That sounds like a broad generalization, but it is not.

A couple of months ago I interviewed a man who is now in hiding, Baruch Marzel, the leader of the fanatical group to which the mass-murderer Baruch Goldstein belonged. The organization is called Kach, which means simply 'thus'. The name is presumably meant to express cold logic, and Mr Marzel's logic is very cold indeed. 'In Jewish law,' he said, 'there is no turning the other cheek. Arab attacks are met with retaliation. There are no such things as innocent victims. The Arabs of Hebron all support terrorist groups, so all are terrorists. They all want to kill me, so I will kill them first.' Under the peace deal, a Palestinian police force is planned. By Mr Marzel's definition all the police will be terrorists, so he will shoot them on sight. God gave this land to the Jews, therefore the Arabs – a million of them – must be removed. The policy is called 'transfer'. Marzel is a fanatic, a racist (and proud of it), but he is not an outcast among the settlers. Many see the mass-murderer Goldstein as a martyr, an avenger, carrying out a biblical injunction to smite the enemies of the Jews.

The settlers who came to Hebron were the first into the occupied territories after the 1967 war. Since then, and feeding on the excuse given them by murderous Palestinian attacks, they have proclaimed the cult of the strong Jew, and imposed an arrogant, strutting, armed vigilantism on the Arab city with the connivance of the army and successive governments including, to its shame, this one. The result was the Hebron massacre. The Palestinians cannot return to the peace table unless the Israelis make significant amends. The gesture that would unlock the door to peace, and a way out of the massacre crisis, is the evacuation of Jewish settlers from the heart of Hebron.

This is probably too radical, even too logical, but it is on the agenda for the first time. Up to half, maybe even a majority, of the cabinet are said to support it. But the one who matters is Mr Rabin, and he is a very cautious man. He did, however, in one leap, dispense with one load of dogma he inherited from the previous government: he recognized the PLO. That done, and with both sides in effect accepting the two-state solution, it would have been relatively easy to reach an agreement were it not for the settlements: a time-bomb planted by the right-wing government of Shamir and Sharon to blow up under Rabin's peace policy.

If the massacre galvanizes Mr Rabin into some cold logic of his own − removal of the irritant, of the obstacle to peace, the Hebron settlements − then the bomb will have gone off prematurely. But if he does not take on the settlers who hate him, hate the Arabs, hate the peace, then Baruch Goldstein, the fanatic who − in the name of God − slaughtered people at prayer, may have succeeded in destroying the peace.

FEAR IN ALGIERS

ALFRED HERMIDA   ALGIERS   24 MARCH 1994

After the Algerian military cancelled the 1992 elections, which the Islamic Salvation Front had been poised to win, political killings, violence and intimidation became everyday activities in Algiers. The city's residents attempted to lead normal lives amid forecasts of civil war and a takeover by Muslim fundamentalists.

The Algerian playwright Abdelkader Alloula was walking to a cultural centre to give a talk when a young man called out his name. Alloula turned round to exchange greetings, and found himself facing two armed men. Seconds later he was on the ground, bleeding from two bullet wounds in the head. He died a few days later, never emerging from a coma. Alloula was just another of the intellectuals to die in the wave of assassinations being carried out by Islamic radicals in Algeria. It is part of a campaign of terror designed to undermine confidence in the government. The streets have become the new killing ground: anyone who has anything to do with the state is in danger. Doctors, schoolteachers and journalists have all met their end at the hand of militants.

People do not even feel safe at home – several prominent personalities have been slaughtered in their own living-rooms. Fleeing the violence, hundreds have escaped into neighbouring Morocco or Tunisia, or to the former colonial master, France. Those still in the country get through the days as best they can. One journalist told me that he and his wife were on tranquillizers, while they planned to leave the country with their two daughters. Algerians can not help feeling that the situation is spiralling out of control; parts of the country have become no-go areas for the security forces and are in the hands of Islamic militias.

Geographically, Algeria lends itself to guerrilla warfare. Its large

142

mountainous expanses provide a natural hiding place for militants, and some thirty years ago nationalist fighters used the mountains as their base for raids against the occupying French forces. Now Islamic radicals are using the same tactics against the generals running the country, and they are not afraid to show their strength. The militants have brazenly set up their own road-blocks, even in the capital itself. In towns like Blida, to the south of Algiers, they have taken over the role of the local authorities. Earlier in the week Blida was a ghost town, after militants ordered shopkeepers to close early and told people to stay off the streets. In such fundamentalist strongholds, most women cover their hair with a scarf, at the demand of the militants. A seventeen-year-old who refused to submit to their demands was killed, as an example to others.

The government, meanwhile, appears oblivious to what is happening around it. Ministers continue to talk of the need to secure order and stability, either by all-out repression or through negotiations. But the regime is paralysed by divisions over which path to pursue, and is instead half-heartedly taking both and failing completely. Government inertia is simply fuelling the discontent that gave rise to the Islamic fundamentalist movement in the first place. The fundamentalists' message of social justice touched a nerve among the young men who lined the streets of Algiers, propping up the wall, smoking or drinking coffee. They have no jobs and no prospect of employment. Home is usually a dingy one-bedroom flat, which they share with the rest of their family. In areas like Bab el Oued in the capital, it is not uncommon to hear of a family of nine living in two rooms and sleeping in shifts.

The queues for bread start early in Bab el Oued. The loaves are snapped up quickly, as no one knows whether there will be bread tomorrow. Other everyday goods like oil and sugar are also in short supply, and when they are available, they are expensive. Algerians have seen the purchasing power of their dinar shrink as the government tries to move from a state economy to a free-market system. But while prices have gone up, wages have remained the same. The average monthly salary of £150 does not go far in Algeria these days – even the most basic goods are expensive, like rice at £1 for a pound. After years of state control, the economy has all but ground to a halt. The price of Algeria's socialist dream has been factories working at half their rate, with employees who think the government owes them a living. The only part of the economy that works is the black market, which is free-market capitalism gone wild. Margaret Thatcher would be proud of the young men who regularly cross to Europe by plane or ferry and return loaded down with Italian designer jeans, Swiss chocolate and French cheese. In the old town in Algiers, the Kasbah, shops openly display goods smuggled into the country. Diplomats estimate that the black market makes up 20 per cent of the economy, all of it outside the control of the state and, of course, paying no taxes.

Like most Algerians, diplomats in Algiers believe it is only a matter of time before the Islamic fundamentalists take power. 'I would not put any money on the government lasting until the end of the year,' a senior diplomat told me, 'although I would risk a tenner on it making it to the summer.' Most Algerians fear a bloodbath once the government falls. Some opponents of the fundamentalists have already started to stockpile weapons in preparation for taking up arms against an Islamic regime. The spectre of civil war is on the horizon, and there appears to be little anyone can do to prevent it.

THE DISAPPEARANCE OF ARAB EAST JERUSALEM

TIM LLEWELLYN   JERUSALEM   28 APRIL 1994

The Israeli and Palestinian peace negotiators still have to reach agreement on Jerusalem, the city both groups want as their capital. But, in the meantime, the Israelis are doing what they can to reduce the influence of the Arabs in what, traditionally, has been their part of the city – East Jerusalem.

Over the quiet, shaded streets of the central part of East Jerusalem there hangs, almost, the atmosphere of an English country town. The Victorian Gothic tower of St George's Anglican Cathedral stares stoically down Salahadin Street towards the Old City of domes and minarets and bell-towers. The explosion of tropical colour in the palm-shaded gardens of the American Colony Hotel is tended with ferocious attention to detail by Valerie Vestor, the English owner, a charming and lively lady who could have escaped, gin and tonic in hand, from the St Mary Mead of Miss Marple; it somehow recalls a small stately home in the Cotswolds. Even Orient House, the PLO's Jerusalem headquarters just around the corner, feels like a Levantine version of a 1950s prep school. Only on the short stroll towards the walled city, past the markets, the service taxi-drivers calling to passengers for the trips to Ramallah, Gaza, Nablus and Hebron, does the Arab world supervene; noisy, chatty, inquisitive, intimate. Through Herod's Gate, towards the Haram al-Sharif or Temple Mount, the Church of the Holy Sepulchre, the Via Dolorosa and the narrow souks, the Muslims, Christians, Jews, Arabs, Armenians and Israelis dwell in resentful congress in the dark interior, a microcosm of the convulsive competitive squabbling of the Middle East.

This weird, oriental agglomeration known as East Jerusalem is under threat. Its unique character is at serious risk as a tide of Israeli concrete laps at its boundaries and slices into and through its centre. Khalil Toufakji, a Palestinian geographer, told me: 'We showed Chairman Arafat a map. We warned him that at the present rate of progress there will soon be no al-Quds, only Urushalayem.' There would be no Arab city, in other words, only a Jewish one. Khalil took me to the Arab suburb of Beit Hanina, three miles up the road, and stood me on a hill to make his point.

To the east we could see the Jewish settlement of Newe Jacob, started in 1967 as soon as Israel occupied the West Bank and annexed East Jerusalem; to our south-east, Pisgat Ze'ev; further south-east, beyond our sight, was the enormous Ma'ale Adumim, with 20,000 Jewish residents and plans for 50,000, straddling the road from Jerusalem to Jericho and Jordan. As far as the eye could see, towards the biblical wilderness, nestling strategically on hilltops, in ranks surrounding Jerusalem and inside East Jerusalem, were the neat white towers of Jewish implants and suburbs, many still being built, with many more still to come. Great highways link these settlements to one another and join them to West Jerusalem and Israel proper, slashing Arab communities apart and surrounding them. To our west, the great sprawling suburb of Ramot edged north, like an urban amoeba, striking deep into the West Bank, its ultimate aim to create yet another Israeli wedge inside Arab land, linking Ramot with the settlement of Givat Ze'ev, which is inching down to meet it.

The Israelis used to confiscate land; now they declare it green belt, refusing Palestinians permission to build on it, yet building on it themselves. All too typically, the settlement of Gilo, with a population of 30,000 in south-east Jerusalem, was built on land confiscated from two Arab villages, Beit Safafa and Beit Jala. The 4,500 Arabs left have little or no land to build on. In the many cases like this in East Jerusalem, Palestinians leave for the West Bank or even further afield, forfeiting or selling their land. Khalil reckons the Palestinians own four square kilometres of land in East Jerusalem, as against seventy-two in 1967. In the past few years, the Jewish population has outstripped the Arabs in East Jerusalem, 150,000 to 140,000, and Israeli institutions like police stations, government offices, the Hebrew University, court-houses, as well as residences and pockets of religious Jews, are liberally distributed through and around the Arab quarter. The plan is to create a 2:1 Israeli majority in East Jerusalem.

In case anyone thought that this juggernaut might have halted after the Rabin–Arafat handshake on the White House lawn last September, 20,000 more Jews have taken up residence in East Jerusalem since then. Jewish expansion in the Muslim quarter of the Old City also proceeds apace. While Yasser Arafat and his aides discuss Gaza and Jericho with the Israelis – endlessly, it seems – in Cairo or elsewhere, the question of the status of Jerusalem, supposedly to be discussed at a later, notional date, is being decided by the planners and builders.

It is not so much a case of urbanization, or even Judaization, or creeping Westernization, as simply one of plain old colonization. When I was there, the Israelis, underlining the isolation and vulnerability of Arab Jerusalem, had cut all roads, major and minor, to the West Bank so that virtually no one from the occupied territories could visit their would-be capital and commercial and spiritual centre. All this violates United Nations Security Council resolutions and the spirit of the peace agreements that the Israelis and their Arab neighbours are so slowly trying to put into effect. Hardly any Palestinians I spoke to can understand what their leaders expect to rule over, to find left, by the time this process is finished, or why they are bargaining about policemen and border controls in Gaza and Jericho when all too soon there will be nothing to police, and nothing to have a border around.

DREAMS OF PARADISE

STEPHEN SACKUR JUBA'A 30 APRIL 1994

As Israeli and Palestinian negotiators spoke of peace, it was easy to forget that the fundamentalist group Hizbollah was still active in the remote hills of southern Lebanon and still waging a campaign of violence against Israeli targets.

Spring brings with it a dazzling kaleidoscope of colours to the hillsides of southern Lebanon. The knee-length meadow grass is awash with wild flowers and the orchards, painstakingly planted in hillside terraces, are laden with blossom. It is strange then to see the trees in the graveyard in the hilltop village of Juba'a, in the heart of an area known in Arabic as the 'region of apples', standing gaunt and leafless, seemingly suspended in permanent mid-winter. Walk up to these grey, miserable trees and they whisper a warning: they tell you of the suffering and bitterness that have infected this beautiful village. A little less than a year ago Juba'a's compact little cemetery was shelled from Israeli artillery positions on the high ridge away to the east. It was an act of deliberate vandalism, an act that left trees and tombstones broken and splintered. Most of the family graves have since been restored, but the trees remain naked and scorched, as dead as the bodies buried next to their roots.

Eighteen-year-old Salma Younes was laid to rest in this melancholy place just a week before my visit. She and her mother were killed instantly when another bout of shelling from the Israeli-occupied area, laughably known as the security zone, reduced their home to rubble. Two adolescent boys showed me her grave, freshly adorned with flowers. The week before Salma was killed she had become engaged to one of their friends, they told me. I asked them what had become of her fiancé and both boys shrugged. 'He's disappeared,' one said. In all probability that grief-stricken youth has already become another recruit for Hizbollah, the Party of God. In Juba'a that is the way things work.

Ever since the Israeli invasion of Lebanon in 1982 this 'region of apples' has been disfigured by constant violence. Israeli troops pulled out of Juba'a in 1985, but they and their allies in the South Lebanese Army hold all the strategic heights to the south and east. The village is an easy and frequent target. Of a pre-war population of 18,000, mostly Shi'ite Muslims, only 5,000 remain and they, almost by definition, are supporters of the Islamic Resistance, the guerrilla fighters of Hizbollah.

The gunmen keep a low profile in the village itself, their presence given away only by their preference for driving around at high speed in Volvo estate cars. Their military operations are conducted in the surrounding hills, where stocks of Iranian-supplied weapons and explosives lie hidden in remote caves and fields. Recruitment to this fighting force runs in families. Anger and hatred, once instilled, are easily passed from brother to brother, from father to son.

Abu Mohammed went on his first active mission with Hizbollah ten years ago. Now in his early forties, he still participates in hit-and-run raids against the nearby positions of the South Lebanese Army. His eldest son, also a fighter, was recently killed, or, as Abu Mohammed would have it, martyred. The spartan, concrete family home is dominated by two photographs: one shows the young man just months before his death, an earnest face with wispy beard pale in the winter sunshine. From the opposite wall comes the stern, unflinching gaze of the late Ayatollah Khomeini, father of Iran's Islamic Revolution and the man who inspired Lebanon's Party of God.

Abu Mohammed, too, is a man of unbending conviction. He used to be a farmer in a nearby village, but now his land is under Israeli control and his farmhouse has been destroyed. The resistance will continue, he told me, until the Israelis and their allies have been removed from every inch of Lebanese soil. His wife, a sturdy woman clothed in layers of black, voices her support. Before every mission she helps him put on his uniform, and hands him a helmet bearing the slogan: 'Victory from God, Liberation Soon'. Abu Mohammed, like all Hizbollah fighters, believes that death on the battlefield is a passport to paradise. The fallen martyrs, he explained, inhabit a beautiful land of green valleys, high mountains and sparkling rivers. It sounded like a description of southern Lebanon in a different, more peaceful era.

For the Israelis the stubborn resistance presented by Hizbollah in Juba'a and other frontline villages is a constant source of frustration. In recent weeks remote-controlled roadside bombs planted by Abu Mohammed and his colleagues have killed several senior officers in the South Lebanese Army and have terrified the Lebanese civilian population inside the security zone. One senior Israeli intelligence officer described Hizbollah to me as an 'efficient terrorist machine' controlled by Iran. 'There will be no comprehensive Middle East peace', he said, 'unless the governments in Beirut and Damascus put a stop to Hizbollah's military activities.' The statement provides its own telling commentary on the achievements of Israeli policy in Lebanon in the last twelve years. The Israelis invaded their northern neighbour in order to end, once and for all, guerrilla attacks on their border settlements. In so doing they created an environment in which Islamic militancy, backed by Iranian money and weapons, could thrive as never before.

For all the talk of a new era in the Middle East, of compromises based on 'land for peace', the vicious local war in south Lebanon is far from over. At the bottom of the graveyard in Juba'a is an area reserved for Hizbollah martyrs. Tombstones adorned with pictures and personal possessions have been placed in the little square. Around the plot coloured ribbons snap and hum in the stiff breeze. Abu Mohammed's son is here, along with almost twenty other local men. There is, of course, still space for others who dream of paradise.

ALL EYES ON GAZA

ALEX BRODIE   GAZA   7 MAY 1994

After the euphoria surrounding the White House handshake between Israeli Prime Minister Yitzhak Rabin and PLO Chairman Yasser Arafat, disenchantment set in. The peace process seemed to be moving at snail's pace, despite a follow-up signing ceremony in Cairo.

No one approaching the Erez checkpoint between Israel and the Gaza Strip can have any doubt that this is a hostile frontier. There are the watchtowers – square, high, prison-camp structures – the floodlights, barriers, guns, surveillance, suspicion, and the new fence. The self-rule fence, high and made of wire, is being laid along the 25-mile length of the Gaza Strip to keep the Arabs of Gaza in. For this peace deal is not about coexistence, it's about separation. After one of the futile and bloody explosions of tribalism that punctuate this conflict – I can't remember which one, there have been so many – the Israeli writer and peace activist, Amos Oz, wrote in exasperation that if two peoples couldn't live together in a civilized manner then they would have to be separated and a wall built between them. There is now a wall separating Gaza and Israel.

Perhaps the deal signed this week in Cairo will ultimately be seen as the beginning of an enduring peace between neighbours, as the opening of a new book, not just a new chapter in the old one. But idealistic dreams of coexistence are for the future. What we have now is a messy, unsatisfactory experiment which contains within it the seeds of its own destruction, but which just has to work for the sake of peace. Israelis see Gaza as many Britons see Northern Ireland – they wish they could just tow it out to sea and sink it. Yitzhak Rabin and Shimon Peres, Israel's septuagenarian leaders, are trying to do the next best thing, get out and leave Gaza to Yasser Arafat.

Israel has withdrawn from Gaza twice before: in 1948 after a brief invasion – Rabin was there as a young brigade commander – and in 1957, after the Suez campaign. Shimon Peres described the ten years that followed, when Israel was free of Gaza, as the quietest decade in the country's history. He was adamant that the third withdrawal would be the last, that Israel would not go back. If he wants that to be true, then Palestinian self-rule has to work, or chaos and anarchy will spill over into Israel. The key is obviously to improve the living conditions of the people – and that will be a huge task.

It is a remarkable contrast passing through the Erez checkpoint, going from the irrigated, symmetrical, cultivated fields of Israel into the ramshackle, dusty Third World: pot-holed roads, litter and plastic blown against the fruit trees, refuse everywhere and precious little living space, especially in the refugee camps. Jabaliya is the biggest of these. Goats, dogs and chickens nose through piles of stinking rubbish, next to stalls of fruit. Ancient Peugeot cars fume and rattle around the donkey-carts, animals and people clutter the dust tracks which wind through a shanty town of corrugated iron and breeze-block shacks and wooden market stalls. When it rains, the dust turns to the most glutinous mud. Once, in a storm, I watched the streets of Gaza become rivers of black water, which poured out of the city over the cliff and into the sea, turning it black. There are worse things than open drains – so long as they're not all clogged.

In the middle of the city is a patch of ground the size of a football pitch – indeed that's what it must have been once, for there's a metal goal-post standing above every manner of twisted debris and refuse, poking above the surface of a stagnant lake of foul-smelling water. Even at the height of summer there's standing water that never drains away. In the slums of Gaza there's no open space, only waste ground. Here, Israel's bitterest foes are bred. Here, Israel's soldiers, sweating in their flak-jackets, tramp scared and scorned, taunted by kids. Only their guns are respected. Here, Israel's soldiers become brutalized – shooting stone-throwing children does nothing for the morale of a modern army.

If Yitzhak Rabin can disentangle his army from this, most Israelis will thank him for it. But it won't be enough. Self-rule in Gaza and Jericho alone will not bring the Israelis peace with the Palestinians, because Gaza is only half the Palestinian nation under Israeli occupation, and only a bit of the land. It must spread to the rest of the occupied territories. For although peace with the Palestinians is not the most important thing to Rabin's government, it is a necessary prelude to the real aim – a comprehensive peace with the Arab neighbours, Jordan, Lebanon, and, most importantly, Syria. Israeli policy-makers fear that if there is no peace with Syria, there will be another war. Israel's nightmare of just a few years in the future is a rebuilding of the eastern front against it – this time with Syria, Iraq and Iran armed with nuclear missiles. To break the Arab wall confronting it, Israel must make peace with Syria. To do that, it has to settle with the Palestinians, and it is starting with self-rule in Gaza. It had better work.

DISUNITED YEMEN

SIMON INGRAM   YEMEN   21 MAY 1994

Enmity between Yemen's president and his dismissed vice-president led to an unconventional, yet violent, civil war in which Scud missiles were used. As ever, it was the non-combatants, the ordinary Yemenis, who were the victims.

We left for the battlefront before dawn: four journalists and two Defence Ministry minders were crammed uncomfortably into the back of an army Toyota Land Cruiser. Under our feet was a pile of newspapers; we weren't just going to report the news, we were going to deliver it as well. At each remote checkpoint on the mountain road, south of Sana'a, the chief minder in the front seat would thrust several copies of the paper into the hands of the waiting sentry. By lunch-time we'd reached al-Dalaa, scene of the great victory reported triumphantly by Sana'a Radio the previous day. The town itself seemed miraculously unscathed. A large number of men carrying Kalashnikovs were milling about near a café, but in Yemen a man without a gun is the exception rather than the rule, even in peacetime.

We drove on until a battered T-55 tank appeared on the road ahead, its gun-barrel pointing over a ridge into a deep valley below. A group of soldiers from the Northern Hamza Brigade wandered over. It had been a fierce battle, they said, but everything was quiet now. That much was apparent from the pair of bare feet sticking out from under the tank. The commander explained that his men had had little sleep in almost a week of fighting. The slur in his voice, however, had less to do with fatigue than with the lump the size of a golf ball protruding from his left cheek. The chewing of the narcotic leaf known as *khat* is a universal addiction in Yemen, and neither army has permitted a mere war to interfere with its ritual afternoon pastime. By dusk each day the drug has done its work, and across the

154

battlefront the cannons open up with renewed ferocity. The *khat* factor is just one oddity of this most unconventional of wars. Away from the propaganda barrage of claim and counter-claim, few things are what they seem.

Another gruelling Land Cruiser ride took us to Shabwa province, 400 kilometres east of Sana'a, where, we had been told, forces loyal to the president had secured another decisive blow against the secessionist rebels. A visit to the village of Baihan suggested otherwise. The army was nowhere in sight, and our party was rapidly surrounded by several hundred heavily armed tribesmen, each determined to recount his part in the battle to the world's media. Local pride was thankfully satisfied with some posed photographs outside a weapon store, abandoned the day before by the Southern forces, who had fled without a fight. Our minder, meanwhile, helped himself to two boxes of Russian-made machine ammunition, which we dropped off at his uncle's home on our way back to Sana'a.

Bizarre episodes like this make it hard at times to take this war entirely seriously, which may explain why it comes as such a shock to be confronted with its essential brutality. Being on the receiving end of all too real shell-fire, during the battle for the southern base of al-Anad, was one such moment, as was watching rescue workers dig bodies out of the rubble of a house in Sana'a following a Scud missile attack. Then there were the things we were not allowed to see, like the arrest of several thousand supporters of the Southern Socialist Party, whose fate, for the moment, can only be guessed at. There were the threats that had silenced a once independent media: the editor of the English-language *Yemen Times* was told that he would be shot unless he stopped publication. Then, from time to time, the clash of cultures that lies at the heart of the conflict comes to the surface.

In the socialist stronghold of al-Dalaa I watched Northern soldiers smash cases of vodka and beer looted from a hotel, the air ringing with cries of 'God is great!' The same day, government newspapers in Sana'a described how loyal citizens were engaged in acts of moral purification, burning Marxist manuals found in captured Southern towns. The divide between conservative, tribal-based North Yemeni society and the more open secular South is, of course, nothing new. Unification almost exactly four years ago only papered over the differences. Military conquest, were President Saleh to achieve it, would not settle matters either. The only conclusion to be drawn is that this war will have no winners, and that the biggest losers will be the Yemeni people. In this, one of the world's poorest countries, ordinary Yemenis tell you they still believe in unity. However, they can only watch in despair as two quarrelling leaders pull their dreams apart.

FIVE YEARS AFTER KHOMEINI

MONICA WHITLOCK   TEHRAN   23 JUNE 1994

The death in 1989 of Ayatollah Khomeini, the father of Iran's Islamic Revolution, is commemorated each year by a period of official mourning. This year our correspondent was among a group of foreign journalists who were invited to attend. It gave her the opportunity to assess the state of the Iranian revolution five years on.

On the eve of Ayatollah Khomeini's anniversary, the lounge of the old Sheraton Hotel in Tehran was full of smart young couples eating ice-cream sundaes. Gathered under an old plastic 'Down With USA' sign, they came, as they come every night, to eye one another's clothes, to show off their children in their velvet frocks and lacy collars, and to mull over the latest rumours. Behind the scenes, a discreet tape played old piano favourites: 'Smoke Gets in Your Eyes' and 'Moonlight on the Water'. The occasional black banner flapped in the street, the Ministry of Slogans had added a few new paintings to the walls and bus drivers displayed little posters of Khomeini in their windows. But there was little conviction in the air. In the hot night of downtown Tehran, the neon pizza bars were open and teenagers cruised in cars more or less ignored by the armed gangs of boys who check passers-by for un-Islamic behaviour. Tehran is huge, jammed with traffic and out of control. Fumes from millions of decrepit car exhausts mix with dust and industrial smoke to cloak the city in a permanent smog. The trees that line the old avenues are pitted and dying. Before the Islamic Revolution, about four million people lived here. Now, there are more than three times as many. Thirty years ago, wolves and foxes roamed the remote region of Vanak; it's in the middle of town now, where the Sheraton stands.

157

The south of the city heaves with slums while home-made shacks sprawl out in all directions up the hillsides, tapping a little electric power from the factories. More families arrive every day, hoping for jobs and a better life. But the city is already stretched far beyond its capacity: teachers, and even professional soldiers, drive taxis or make kebabs in the evening to make ends meet. Countless half-baked building projects have been abandoned, leaving only scaffolding. There's no planning, no social security; if you're destitute, the family must provide, as it always has. But visit any family in Tehran and you will be told that it's not just the city that has changed, it's the people. 'We've turned in on ourselves,' I was told again and again. People may go out to show off the latest way to get around the dress codes: shoes dripping with artificial pearls, or lycra leggings under the *hejab*. Teenagers may go strolling in the park, away from watchful parents. But most people feel safer at home nowadays. 'We have to watch what we say,' I was told, 'and we don't know whom to trust.'

Even staying at home is risky. The neighbours may well not inform the authorities if you have a little party, but they might – you can't be sure. Besides, the sight of too many cars in the street is a dead giveaway. Alcohol is easy enough to get hold of, but it's hard to relax with a glass of home-made vodka when you can't be sure who's outside the door. Even television is dangerous; owning a video-player is legal but most of the films worth watching are not. Some parents boast about how well they have taught their children to lie at school about life at home. 'She's so clever,' they say, 'she's only eight and she says: "Daddy reads the Koran in the evening".' Others feel guilty and sickened, and despair over the hollow future of a generation brought up to hide the truth about the simplest, everyday things.

From thousands of roofs across Teheran, satellite TV beams visions of the outside world into thousands of living rooms. The most popular channels present a bizarre muddle of Arab belly-dancing, misty pop videos from Glasgow, and nameless sports that look more like nameless sex. It all merges into one after a while, nothing like as startling as catching sight of a woman in a Tehran street with bare ankles. Watching satellite TV may soon join playing backgammon and not wearing socks on the neurotic list of prohibited activities in Iran. On an ordinary day, you can break the law from dawn to dusk, often unwittingly. Tehranis are expert at stretching the better-known rules: everyone knows where to buy or sell a few black-market Swiss francs, or a video, or a bottle of smuggled whisky, and many palms can be crossed with a few dollars. 'We just get on with our lives,' one man said to me, 'it doesn't make any difference whether it's the Shah or Khomeini or this lot in charge.' Fiddling the rules is a way of life, and a sad and hollow way to consume the vision and energy of so many millions of people.

ASIA AND THE PACIFIC

THE BODY POLITIC

BRIAN BARRON   MANILA   11 SEPTEMBER 1993

The former dictator of the Philippines, Ferdinand Marcos, was buried back in his home province seven years after being ousted from power and forced to leave the country. But although his departure then was tainted by allegations against him of brutality and corruption, his family continued to enjoy a considerable following.

One of Hitchcock's finest comedy thrillers has Cary Grant clambering precariously among the colossal stone heads carved from Mount Rushmore in the American West. I was reminded of that dizzy climax while on a solo ascent of the most ludicrous relic from the twenty-year rule of Ferdinand Marcos, 'F.M.' to his cronies. It is an enormous head of F.M., at least fifty feet high, dominating a hillside near Baguio City. You are not supposed to touch the monolith, let alone circumnavigate one lofty cheek, but as I clambered past F.M.'s gigantic nostrils, scrabbling for handholds, the reason for the 'Keep Off' signs became clear. Far from being hewn from some ancient rock, like Ozymandias, King of Kings, F.M.'s countenance is an unstable mix of chicken-wire netting and cement of dubious quality. I retreated lest one footfall too many brought terminal collapse. But this now-neglected site, above what is still called the Marcos Highway, typifies the *folie de grandeur* of F.M. and his tireless widow, Imelda Marcos.

In boutique black, somehow both sorrowful and strong-jawed, flanked by her tearful offspring, Imelda Marcos has offered compelling theatre during these recent funeral days. If this cult of the dead offends those of puritan ethic, remember that this is an archipelago besieged by earthquakes, volcanoes and hurricanes in which myths, cults and paganism sprout like jungle creepers. For this past week Imelda Marcos cast herself in the role of high priestess. The crowds stayed away; it is a long way from Manila to the Marcos home province of Ilocos Norte. But there is a grudging respect for Mrs Marcos's sheer willpower. Not long ago she was reviled, along with her dead husband, as the biggest thief in modern Asia's history. The hoi polloi slapped their thighs and fell about when they saw the presidential palace, with her 500 abandoned brassieres and 3,000 pairs of shoes. But now the embattled widow, still under indictment for allegedly looting the national coffers, can be seen as a doughty fighter for her own family, a widow doing the Christian thing for her husband's remains. Filipinos, protective of their extended family network, are a sentimental, God-fearing lot enduring threadbare conditions.

The roller-coaster life of Imelda, the one-time local beauty queen who hit the jackpot, strikes a familiar chord. A society that was once an American colony now cherishes Hollywood hype and speaks in a patois that borrows heavily from 77 Sunset Strip. Mrs Marcos's tinsel-town values are the stuff of dreams. Perhaps that's why the wonderfully named Cardinal Sin, Archbishop of Manila, thunders from the pulpit against those giving funeral honours to a president who brought terror and dictatorship. Cardinal Sin worries that his flock is too trusting.

That reminds me of a first assignment in Manila twenty-four years ago. At that time it was, in effect, a Wild West town improbably anchored in the South China Sea. For personal survival, just about everyone carried a gun; if you dined with Filipino friends, they would leave their revolvers with the receptionist. There was prohibition, so wine was poured out of a teapot into teacups. F.M. in person proved fluent, charismatic, handsome; not a grey hair in sight although he was well into middle age. His philandering was legendary. Manila's best-selling audio-tape purported to be a secret recording of the president making love to his young American mistress and finally singing to her. Over the finale the producers of this black-market production had dubbed boogie-woogie music. The overall effect was hilarious, but no one doubted the tape's authenticity. Indeed, there was much macho approval.

As time passed, Marcos's despotism grew. Death-squads appeared. The word 'salvaging', meaning the killing of Marcos opponents, entered the national vocabulary. From being one of Asia's promising fledgling democracies, the Philippines became a banana republic. So today F.M., waxed and pomaded by the republic's finest embalmer, lying snugly inside a lacquered casket, has a lot to answer for. His legacy is the melancholy fact that the Philippines is far behind its industrious neighbours. There is still a hard core of partisans who benefited enough to convince themselves that F.M. was a genius. There are even lunatic cults, like the College of Mystery, which worship Marcos as a God. The odds are that eventually the body politic now parked in an air-conditioned mausoleum in F.M.'s home province will be allowed into Manila for some kind of state funeral. But that could take some time: by then Imelda Marcos may have joined him in a mink-lined paradise.

THE CHAIRMAN'S
BODYGUARD OF LIES

BRIAN BARRON HONG KONG
26 DECEMBER 1993

*On Boxing Day 1993 communist China celebrated the centenary
of the birth of Chairman Mao Zedong, guerrilla commander,
visionary, poet, revolutionary leader – and philanderer.
Disclosures on BBC television about his womanizing and his
savage treatment of Communist Party comrades who crossed him
angered the Chinese government.*

One mile from my base in Hong Kong is Hollywood Road, hidden
away behind the phalanx of skyscrapers guarding Victoria Harbour.
Among the scores of oriental antique shops there, offering everything
from Tang dynasty tomb guardians to Ching porcelain pillows, is a
window in which a life-size figure shrouded in a military greatcoat
raises an arm as if saluting the knick-knack shoppers. This replica of
the Great Helmsman, carved during the height of the Cultural Revolution twenty-five years ago, is priced at an intimidating £45,000.
For the local battalion of Chinese tycoons keen to polish their patriotic credentials, that is pocket-money. When we asked permission to
film the statue we were politely rebuffed: 'No publicity, thank you.
We don't want problems from Westerners making fun of our Chairman
Mao.'

As we have seen from Beijing's recent statements, the instinct to
protect Mao's reputation is not confined to opportunistic Hong Kong
Chinese eyeing the end of British rule in 1997. Unlike Stalin, Mao
has never been demythologized. In the West today one can still find
lingering admiration for Maoist achievements, especially among those
who were students at the time of protests – like Paris 1968 – which

sought to mimic the Cultural Revolution. An added irony is that Mao, the iconoclast, is now a pop icon of the late twentieth century. The ruling clique in Beijing today is wedded to the fiction of Mao Zedong, the only-slightly-flawed demigod. The Communist Party, shorn of idealism, governing a deeply cynical society careering towards capitalist market practice, needs Mao as the totem-pole to justify its monopoly of power.

A few weeks ago in a Chicago suburb I interviewed Dr Li Sui Zhi, the exiled physician whose disclosures about Mao's paranoia and womanizing have incensed Beijing. The doctor is a dignified old charmer who was hand-picked to be the Chairman's doctor in 1954. Obssessive security in Beijing prevented him from having other patients. At first, as a patriotic Chinese, Dr Li worshipped his employer, spellbound by Mao's leadership skills, his scholarship in the Chinese classics, his earthy wisdom and humour. Mao had no close friends, and he deliberately stayed aloof from the rest of the politburo. But he loved talking: most days, for twenty-two years, the doctor listened to Mao unfiltered by the usual screen of party minders and propagandists. As the 1950s rolled into the 1960s, however, Dr Li felt he had seen and heard too much.

Daily life in a threadbare China lurched from one purge and crisis to the next as Mao, who despised routine and dreamed of endless revolution, devised new political campaigns to indoctrinate and mobilize the masses. The fact that these brought disasters – such as the famine in which millions died following a madcap rush to industrialization called the Great Leap Forward – did not affect the Chairman's composure. It was, after all, Mao the ultimate realist who remarked that a revolution was not a dinner party. Without sacrifice, no revolution could be successful. What emerges from Dr Li's unique insights within Beijing's leadership compound is the fact that by the early 1960s Mao had been shunted to the margins of power, blamed for China's economic failures. As Mao later remarked: 'I was treated with respect but like an aged relative at a funeral.' To turn the tables on his opponents, he invented the Cultural Revolution. By inciting millions of students to become Red Guards he blew apart the Communist Party from within. In the years of turmoil and Chinese chauvinism that followed spy-mania flourished, children were taught to betray their parents and torture and killing engulfed China. At that time the West had only flickering glimpses of the chaos, which was ended by deploying the People's Liberation Army.

By 1968 Mao was stronger than any emperor in China's 4,000 years of authoritarian history. The Chinese people were bombarded by what his party zealots called 'thought rectification'. A book from that period, entitled *The Miracles of Chairman Mao*, is crammed with testimonies about his amazing talents. Here is a typical quote from Beijing Radio, dated 6 February 1969, describing a naval rescue: 'As the rescue craft approached the sinking fishing boat, the commander shouted through a megaphone: "Comrade fishermen, Chairman Mao has sent us to bring you back." The fishermen were moved to tears. They waved their Little Red Books of quotations from Chairman Mao to greet their rescuers. Cheers of "Chairman Mao is great" and "A long long life to Chairman Mao" rang out across the Eastern Sea.'

As a struggling revolutionary Mao denounced the cult of the individual. It was, he said, a rotten carry-over from the history of mankind. Decades later, when Mao as infallible leader was asked by a foreign friend why he had sanctioned a personality cult that out-shone even that of Kublai Khan, the Chinese leader cited the overthrow of Krushchev in the Soviet Union. Mao's point was that if Krushchev had had a personality cult he too might have been invulnerable.

Of all the stories recounted by the doctor, the most fascinating was not the detailed descriptions of Mao's dalliance with young concubines, but the dying Chairman's words in 1976. Mao clutched Dr Li's hand and whispered: 'Is there any hope?' Wisely, the doctor said that there was. 'Good,' said Mao, and died moments later. What a convincing climax. It shows Mao desperate to hang on to life, just like the rest of us. But he died as the Red Emperor of China. Surely, seventeen years on, he does not need a bodyguard of lies?

PEKING DOG

JAMES MILES   BEIJING   22 JANUARY 1994

The economic boom in China has brought its people a greater amount of disposable income than they have enjoyed before. Many Chinese are choosing to spend their cash on dogs to keep as pets, despite the fact that dog ownership is illegal.

When I stopped to ask the way to the dog-market in Beijing's eastern suburbs, a man told me it had been closed down. 'It's tense,' he warned. But in spite of his advice, I persevered and eventually found it by the side of a dirty, half-frozen canal. The atmosphere was indeed tense. A few shifty men stood by an equal number of puppies. This, they claimed, was the only dog-market left in the neighbourhood. Several others had been closed down by the police, and all the dogs confiscated. The animals on display by the canal were just the cheaper specimens; they cost £20 or £30 each. It wasn't long, however, before the traders produced the real goods from under their thick padded overcoats: fluffy little lap-dogs, Pekinese and Shih-tzus. These, they said, cost £100 or £200. Then they stuffed them quickly back inside their coats, out of sight of any passing policemen. They could show me dogs costing £1,000 or £2,000 if I cared to go with them, they said – dogs smuggled into China by train from Russia, by air from Japan and boat from South Korea.

As official newspapers here put it, dog-fever is sweeping the country. For the newly rich – and this is a fast-growing class in China – owning a dog is now the way of flaunting one's wealth. Never mind the fact that in Beijing, and most other cities, dog owner-ship is illegal. Admittedly, these last few days have been tough. Not only have the authorities been closing down dog-markets, but, say residents, officials have even been raiding homes, seizing pet dogs and beating them to death. Some citizens seem unperturbed, like the soldier I saw this week, in his olive-green fatigues, leading a distinctly un-military-looking pooch along a busy street. Officially, dogs are banned for reasons of hygiene, perhaps reasonably given that thousands of people every year die of rabies in China. But there's clearly a political motive, too. Owning a dog, except for practical purposes, is seen as simply too bourgeois. As the party newspaper, the *People's Daily*, put it in a blistering commentary earlier this month: 'How can we have pet dogs when our country is still in the initial stages of socialism and some rural areas are only just emerging from poverty?'

These days, however, few people pay much attention to the *People's Daily*. The closure of a few dog-markets notwithstanding, huge numbers of people are buying dogs. One newspaper claimed that a dog had been sold in the capital of Sichuan Province for more than £23,000. A columnist in the *China Daily* newspaper said that a dog-owning friend of his was now ashamed to be seen in public with his pet, because it had only cost something in the region of £50. In China, that's about two months' wages for the average city-dweller. The same columnist said that dogs in China were consuming as much grain as 40 million people. But while the media fulminate, dog hospitals, dog beauty parlours and shops selling food and clothing for the creatures are springing up in the cities. Just down the road from the BBC office in Beijing is a place called the KPK World Pet Zoo, a Hong Kong-owned establishment offering round-the-clock medical services, hair-styling and imported dog-food. 'Doggie-do Salon, Style and Set for Fido,' trumpeted an unusually supportive English-language newspaper in Beijing when the new business was launched late last year. The Chinese media have noted the irony of this dog-worship, given the fondness many Chinese have for eating dogs, especially in winter when dog meat is supposed to have a warming effect. But in the Chinese tradition, the coming lunar new year will mark the start of the Year of the Dog, and so far all the indications point to a year of unprecedented pampering for the once rejected species.

A DAM TOO FAR

CHRISTOPHER GUNNESS   KELANTAN
3 FEBRUARY 1994

A row broke out in the British parliament about the Conservative government's funding of a controversial hydroelectric dam project in Malaysia. Government critics said that in return for the aid, the Malaysians had agreed to buy arms from British companies.

Standing in a sinisterly lit granite cavern resembling a Steven Spielberg set, 1,000 feet under some of the remotest rainforests in the world, it is hard to believe that this is the epicentre of a political earthquake that has erupted in London. But then it is odd how the source of a political crisis is often thousands of miles from the seat of the government it affects. Irangate is a good example, and now Mr Major has his – Floodgate. The allegation is that nearly £250 million of British taxpayers' money was used to fund a dam in the north-east Malaysian state of Kelantan. This may seem philanthropic enough, but allegations have emerged in both Kuala Lumpur and London of an aid-for-guns trade-off. It is being claimed that the British decision to fund the dam was linked to a Malaysian commitment to buy more than £1 billion worth of British weaponry.

To make matters worse for Mr Major it is clear that although, by the standards of South-East Asia, the scheme seems environmentally acceptable, it is literally undermining the ecology of the forest. Looking down from a nearby peak, one sees a huge area of what was the picturesque Pergau River Valley being excavated. The deep emerald of the trees surrounds a huge deforested scar. Acres have been denuded and, say the environmentalists, the result has been siltation of the seven rivers that flow into the Pergau. This reportedly exacerbated the flash-flooding in December in which three people died. In addition, it is claimed in Malaysia that the roads built for the dam have given illegal logging companies access to previously inaccessible areas. You can see small dirt-tracks snaking off into the jungle to where deforestation and subsequent rainfall have washed away the topsoil, revealing acres of granite bedrock.

In addition to the environmental considerations, doubts about the commercial viability of the scheme have been raised. Indeed, senior civil servants in London have said as a matter of public record that electricity produced from the dam will cost the Malaysian taxpayer £100 million more than alternative energy sources would over a thirty-year period. But that is all par for the course when it comes to Western aid, as is the notion that in return for economic assistance Third World countries should buy goods and services from their First World donors. The Anglo-Malaysian trading relationship is a textbook case. Hand in hand with the Pergau dam project has come a mush-rooming of British commerce. Since 1990, British business in Malaysia has tripled: it is now worth about £1 billion a year. Firms are competing for lucrative contracts in an economy which has grown at about 7 per cent a year for the last five years. 'But,' the British taxpayer might ask, 'if our trade has benefited to the tune of many millions, why should we worry?'

The answer is simple. The dam's construction appears to be in violation of Britain's Overseas Aid Act of 1966, which explicitly pro-hibits the linking of military sales with aid allocations. The govern-ment can reply that there has been no explicit linkage, but it must then explain away the fact that since the dam deal was signed, Britain has reportedly sold to Malaysia twenty-eight Hawk trainer aircraft, Marconi air-defence radars, warships and anti-aircraft missiles. It must also explain why British companies are involved in the establishment of two major military training facilities.

In Mr Major's defence, it could be argued that other Western governments, at least those that have such rules, are also breaking them. At times like this, however, it ill behoves a politician to seek refuge in other people's sins. And Mr Major might also argue that if he plays by the rules Britain will lose valuable arms contracts to foreign competition. The economic force of that argument is indeed sobering. For example, with the diminishing of the internal security threat posed by communists in the north, Malaysia is looking to expand its armed forces and, in particular, its navy. This is a sound strategic objective in view of the fact that 85 per cent of Malaysian exports are seaborne and given the necessity of keeping peace in the

South China Sea and Malacca Straits. The Malaysians are looking to buy nearly thirty patrol boats, and shipbuilders from the great sea-faring nations, at least two from Britain, are bidding for the contract. It is the hottest multi-million-pound deal in town, and with the promise of hundreds of potential British jobs, it could be argued that Mr Major needs to be there.

The economic imperative seems overwhelming. However, urgent moral and practical questions remain. Why should Britain give aid to a booming economy like Malaysia when other, more needy cases are overlooked? Is the ultimate aim of aid genuine philanthrophy, or is it really intended to further our commercial interests? If so, why bother with aid at all? One thousand feet below the forests of north-east Malaysia, those questions seem irrelevant. But with some predicting that the ides of March is fast approaching for Mr Major, they are questions that might return to haunt him.

THE PENITENTIARY PIRATES

PETER GODWIN   MANILA   19 FEBRUARY 1994

Piracy, the scourge of a bygone age, is making a comeback. The modern piracy blackspot is the South China Sea off the coast of the Philippines. But because there is so little policing of the ocean, very few of the new pirates are caught. Peter Godwin paid a visit to Manila prison in search of that rare species, the pirate in captivity.

Manila Penitentiary stands on a hill overlooking the city. It is actually more of a town than a prison: it has suburbs, parks, schools, shops, farms, street markets and buses. In fact, it works far more smoothly than the rest of Manila. It is an island of sanity in the capital of chaos. Mr Misar is the prison director, just as his father was before him. Misar senior is now immortalized in a mini-Mount Rushmore-style sculpture carved into a modest limestone cliff at the prison entrance. He would be proud of his son, a taut little sparrow of a man marching about in his tennis whites. Everywhere Mr Misar goes, people snap to attention: warders, prisoners, visitors, even casual passers-by. According to his penal philosophy, Mr Misar is a liberal. He believes that reform, not punishment, is the priority of the prison. When he interviews inmates he holds one of their hands in both of his, rather like a kindly parish priest.

The director's mansion – all high ceilings and hardwood floors, potted ferns and a baby grand piano – stands at the end of a long avenue of acacia and avocado trees. The director's wife gets up from her bridge rubber to bid us welcome. She is a vision of some 1950s middle-American dream, with her butterfly spectacles, a tent-dress and an off-white poodle at her side. A short stroll from the director's

174

mansion, more than five thousand of the most dangerous men in the Pacific area are incarcerated in the maximum-security wing. It is a curious edifice, with the facade of a Beau Geste fort and summery blue-striped awnings over the entrance. Inside, however, there is an altogether grimmer scene. In the visitors' waiting room there is a large display cabinet in which, neatly arranged, is a gruesome collection of home-made weapons confiscated from the inmates. The sheer ingenuity is astonishing: a pistol made from a bedstead, crossbows, spear-guns with fearsomely barbed arrows, coshes, and every conceivable kind of knife.

Dozens of inmates had crowded behind the bars that separated the waiting room from the main gaol. Their hands reached through the bars, bearing various trinkets for sale: cigarette boxes inlaid with mother-of-pearl and miniature sailing boats in bottles. Cecilio Chanco, alias Bobo the Pirate, was finally ushered in. But it soon became clear that he had changed his mind. When we had last spoken to him, a month before, he had been keen to tell his true story and to plead his innocence to the world. Since then he had clearly realized that piracy was sexy, that robbing a boat had magically elevated him above his prosaic fellow murderers, robbers, rapists and arsonists. This little man in baggy khaki shorts and flip-flops had, he announced portentously, been interviewed by *Playboy* and by the British edition of *GQ* magazine. He now had a London-based agent, he went on, through whom all deals would have to be negotiated.

None of the four other members of his pirate gang would talk either, he assured us – but we decided to try anyway. Prisoners were dispatched, at five pesos a go, to track them down. The search brought back only one – Roger Tullin, described in court documents as the principal seajacker of a ship called the *Tabangao*. As it happened, Tullin had not been signed up by *Playboy* and was anxious to talk. I questioned him in English but Tullin insisted on replying in dialect, in a hoarse whisper, with one eye constantly on the prison guards, who were straining to overhear our curious interchange. When we translated the television interview later, we discovered that Tullin had been trying to tell me details of his torture. It makes deeply embarrassing viewing. After each of his replies there is a hearty response from me as, ignorant of his remarks, I try to jolly him along.

Our final stop on the prison tour was the chamber of death. On the day of our visit the Filipino government had approved the introduction of the death sentence for what were described as 'six heinous crimes', including piracy. Luckily for Roger Tullin and Bobo Chanco, the legislation was not retrospective. There may be a practical problem implementing it, anyway: the last time they tried to execute someone in the electric chair here it short-circuited, and the whole chamber went up in flames. Now death row stood abandoned in the twilight, rusted cell doors ajar, lizards and a bright green snake slithering through the profusion of foliage choking the courtyard.

The death chamber itself, scene of dozens of executions in its day, has been reduced to a blackened shell. The remnants of the electric chair have been removed, but behind its position there was an iron gantry, supporting thick electric cables. Above this the torch beam fell on a large, childish mural of a blindfolded lady of justice, scales in her outstretched hand. When we emerged, it was quite dark. Above us, on the catwalk, in a pool of sodium light, haloed in a dense whirl of insect life, was a guard wearing a pair of Ray-Bans, armed with a shotgun. He looked out over the maximum-security wing where the prisoners groaned and coughed in the darkness of their cells, and beyond them, to the winking neon of Manila, and he whistled the same brittle, cheery tune over and over again.

LAO, PLEASE DON'T RUSH

TIM LUARD   LUANG PRABANG   7 APRIL 1994

Laos's reputation as the least-known and least-developed country in South-East Asia was set to change with the opening of the first bridge across the Mekong River to link Laos to Thailand.

My last visit to Laos had been exactly twenty years ago. People had warned me that I might find some changes, and I did. A medical school now stands on the site of the rambling guesthouse where I had stayed (it had turned out also to be a brothel, but the girls were looking for battle-hardened US soldiers fresh from the Vietnam war across the border rather than student backpackers). Also gone is the opium den down towards the river where, my diary tells me, six pipes used to cost 100 kip, or ten US cents. If that seemed too expensive, there were mounds of marijuana on sale in the morning market.

Last time, I had made the trip up to the old royal capital, Luang Prabang, on the dirt road through the jungle on the roof of a bus. A few days previously, most of the passengers on the bus had been shot dead in an ambush. The attack was blamed by the royalist government on the communist Pathet Lao, which was on the point of seizing power – but it may have been bandits. Either way, you now have to fly up to Luang Prabang. The grass landing-strip at the airport has been given a coat of tarmac, but there is otherwise little sign of change. Monks squat in the shade of mango and papaya trees, in the neatly swept courtyards of a dozen temples. The air is thick with bougainvillaea and incense left over from a festival the night before. The big white building on the corner of the main street has worn well. In 1974 it was the US Information Office, and its windows were regularly shattered in communist attacks. Prior to that it had been a French officers' club. Later, it became the Soviet Cultural Centre. Today, it houses the Laos national tourist agency.

Laos is usually described as being small, remote and landlocked. It's true that it only has four million people. But, in terms of area, Laos is small only if you think of Italy or Britain as small. As for remote and landlocked, it is actually in the middle of the world's two most dynamic economic regions, China and South-East Asia. Some people are beginning to talk in terms of Laos becoming a thriving crossroads and conduit for its neighbours' trade – a future Kuwait or even Hong Kong. But many people in Laos believe the door to the outside world is already open too wide – particularly the front door, to Thailand. Their markets are full of Thai goods and their televisions of Thai programmes, even if their streets are, as yet, still free of Bangkok-style traffic jams.

The new Mekong bridge, a gift from the Australian government, is intended to improve relations between Laos and Thailand. However, I did not meet a single person in Laos who was entirely in favour of it. 'We do not want more pushy Thai businessmen and Western tourists,' they said. 'We do not want to lose our forests and get things like AIDS in return.' The Lao authorities have already used a whole range of methods to slow down the process of change from simple red tape to the outright refusal of licences and visas. At the moment they are wondering whether to try to ban the Thai speedboats which have taken to buzzing up and down the Mekong, disturbing the traditional calm on the right-hand bank.

The Laos have also been resisting Thai attempts to build Luang Prabang a new airport. Last month they finally agreed to sign a contract for the airport, but as I waited in a hut at the side of the runway for my flight, and watched a lone young cyclist dawdling along the narrow strip of tarmac quite oblivious to the arriving plane, I wondered if things might not after all still be much the same in another twenty years. As someone pointed out, Lao People's Democratic Republic – LPDR – also stands for Lao, Please Don't Rush. Someone else pointed out that if you look hard enough you can still find mounds of marijuana in the market, and even the odd opium den down towards the river.

EASTERN VALUES

HUMPHREY HAWKESLEY   BANGKOK
28 APRIL 1994

The row between Britain and Malaysia over the Pergau Dam affair and the caning in Singapore of the American Michael Fay both illustrate a new confidence typical of countries in the Far East. As their economies boom, they are proving increasingly reluctant to listen to advice from Western countries they believe to be in moral decline.

Patricia Hussein has led a rough life around Manchester's red light district. She's separated from her husband. She has two children by other men, and a string of convictions for prostitution. Last week she was arrested at Bangkok airport carrying heroin, and since then she has been experiencing life amid confusing Asian values. At the police station she flirted with officers, cracked jokes and, unlike in Britain, was allowed to wander around the compound. In order to speak to her, we made a small donation to the police stations fund. Patricia, scratching sores on her arms, complained about the filth, the mosquitoes, the sanitation. There's no flush toilet. 'Compared to England, the conditions aren't what I'm used to,' she said. And of course she's right. Patricia Hussein, preparing herself for maybe twenty years in jail, is having to get used to a very different set of moral and cultural values. Whatever you want to call it, it's not like home. This is something that is increasingly being noticed by the West and is having to be addressed: the issue of Asian versus Western values.

In Singapore another young Westerner, Michael Fay, has been sentenced to six strokes of the cane, which could send him into shock and will scar him for life. His crime was spray-painting cars and stealing road signs; a routine act of vandalism in America, but not in

179

Singapore. President Clinton has protested, but Singapore has warned him against imposing American values there. Michael Fay's mother arrived in the spotless city state proclaiming her son's innocence. She went to see him and came out in tears, realizing that her pleas for clemency were getting little sympathy. Meanwhile, radio phone-in shows in the United States showed massive support for the caning. Americans were wondering whether Singapore had got it right after all.

Britain received a similar short, sharp shock in February, when Malaysia banned government trade with British companies. The prime minister, Dr Mahatir Mohammed, had objected to an article in the *Sunday Times* alleging that he was corrupt. The cost to Britain was some £2 billion and 40,000 jobs, according to Minister for Trade Richard Needham.

In the past ten years, a swathe of countries in the Far East have become rich and confident enough to challenge many aspects of Western democracy. They are mostly authoritarian, disciplined one-party states with a controlled press, political prisoners and a repressed opposition. With the exception of Singapore, bribes (commissions or donations, as they are known in the East) are commonplace. Twenty years ago these countries were propped up by aid, terrified of communism and protected by America – factors that were used by the West to win concessions on democracy and human rights.

Today that linkage has been weakened because the economic tigers, as they are called, don't need aid and because the threat of communism has diminished. Indeed, China and Vietnam, the communist stalwarts, have embraced market economics, shelved Marxism, and are looking more similar to their authoritarian and capitalist neighbours. The leaders see themselves as pioneers in a new and successful system of government, where their tough, non-democratic methods have a proven track record. Their countries are relatively crime-free, with high economic growth and little unemployment.

Dr Mahatir, in a recent interview, said that the West had lost its sense of values. 'In New York,' he said, 'you have a beautiful building, then someone comes along with spray paint. People say it's all right, it's an expression of the inner self. We don't want these things to happen here.' His neighbour, Lee Kuan Yew, believes that America is witnessing the breakdown of a civil society where the emphasis is on the right of the individual to misbehave. These are the men who have visions of the Pacific Rim as the economic, perhaps political, force of the twenty-first century; a region bound around the lumbering but developing mass of China. It is becoming so rich that Bill Clinton, whose electoral platform was to get tough over human rights, is having to rethink his policy. Warren Christopher, the secretary of state, was snubbed during his recent visit to Beijing. While he campaigned for human rights, the Chinese police rounded up dissidents. When he threatened trade sanctions, China warned that America had as much to lose – like the contracts and the jobs going to big companies like Boeing.

While businessmen queue up in the marble-pillared lobbies of five-star hotels, the images of Asia, including those of naive Europeans languishing in filthy jails, are changing. There has been little sympathy for Patricia Hussein in Bangkok, and not much for Michael Fay in Singapore. Instead, there's a realization that the style of government here has to be addressed, not criticized. As Dr Mahatir says, the West will have to stop treating him as a tinpot dictator.

ARS LONGA

JAMES MILES   BEIJING   19 MAY 1994

*In communist China, art and politics have always been closely
intertwined. During the rule of Chairman Mao Zedong artists
were allowed only to produce works glorifying the chairman himself
or his totalitarian regime. Since then, there has been some
relaxation of censorship but the authorities remain on their guard.
In an effort to break free of the official strait-jacket, some young
Chinese have left Beijing for the countryside.*

On the north-western outskirts of Beijing, where the city proper
merges into the coutryside beyond, lie the ruins of Yuanmingyuan,
once the Versailles of the Chinese capital. The vast palace, built in
the seventeenth century and designed in Italian baroque style, was
used as the summer retreat of Chinese emperors until it was destroyed
by British and French troops in 1860. Now the shattered marble
columns and the lakes surrounding them form one of the city's best-
loved parks, and it is in a village on the edge of this idyllic expanse
that rebellious young artists have formed their own breakaway community. The village itself is far from idyllic: the stream that runs
through it is clogged with stinking refuse. The rows of brick courtyard
houses are new and characterless. Most of the hundred or so artists
rent tiny rooms with no running water, just big enough for a bed and
a jumble of finished and half-finished works. The peasants who own
the houses make good money out of the bohemian community. Some
of them even insist that the rent is paid in American dollars, knowing
that many of the artists survive by selling their works to foreigners.

The Yuanmingyuan artists' village was founded in the early 1980s
by a group of graduates from Beijing's Central Academy of Fine Arts.
They wanted to pursue their vocation away from the eye of the
authorities, who at that time insisted on the right to assign college

graduates to jobs chosen for them by the government. But it was not until after the violent suppression of the Tiananmen Square protests in 1989 that the village became a Mecca for artists seeking refuge from political and social constraints. A few poets and rock musicians joined them too, transforming the village from an isolated backwater into a bustling settlement with several restaurants.

Two years ago, when the government slightly relaxed its control over the media, at least as far as non-political subjects were concerned, the Chinese media began to publish stories about the artists. The articles mostly portrayed the community as a weird but none the less positive phenomenon. The long hair favoured by the artists particularly fascinated the Chinese press: after a lengthy description of hairstyles in the village, one national daily daringly conceded that long hair could indeed look just as attractive on men as on women. Another newspaper published extracts from the diary of the man unofficially acknowledged by the artists as the mayor of their community, Yan Zhengxue.

Mr Yan, who is in his late forties, said in his diary that the artists had gathered at the village because of the need to remedy the harm caused to art by politics and commercialization. 'We've raised the great flag of rebellion,' he said. 'Although it's possible we'll all be crushed to pieces by this callous society,' he went on, 'we hope that here we'll find our true selves.' When I visited the village a few days ago, young artists eagerly invited me into their cramped dwellings to show off their works. One displayed an unfinished painting of a man and a woman, both naked, standing in front of Mao Zedong's portrait at Tiananmen Square. Another had glued together several ping-pong balls, atop of which was a large rubbery-looking spider.

One artist told me about some friends of his who had staged an exhibition of performance art earlier this year in a room they had hired in central Beijing. On the floor they placed 20,000 books, some in English, some in Chinese. Then they introduced two pigs into the room, one male, the other female. On one of the pigs they had painted what looked like a Chinese character but was not, and on the other what looked like an English word but was not. While the artists videoed the scene, the two pigs copulated and then rootled among the books. Quite what this was supposed to mean, I am not at all sure. Yan Zhengxue was not around during my visit. He had been sentenced without trial in April to two years in a labour camp for allegedly stealing a bicycle and disturbing public order on a bus. The man who had been described by one official newspaper last year as a person whose moral character evoked feelings of profound admiration was now being condemned by the media as a villain. Mr Yan, it appears, made the mistake of trying to do more than break artistic taboos. Last year, he became something of a celebrity in dissident circles for trying to sue a policeman who had beaten him up. Many of his fellow artists as well as political dissidents signed a petition to the government protesting against the police action. The policeman was eventually given a one-year suspended sentence, but the authorities apparently decided that the rebellious Mr Yan should get his come-uppance too. For much of March and April, the artists' village was guarded by police, who prevented foreigners from entering, and although the cordon has now been lifted, some of the artists I spoke to said they feared that their community might soon be broken up by the authorities. They said that most of the artists were vulnerable because they were from other provinces and did not have permits to live in Beijing. Perhaps prophetically, one official newspaper remarked last year that no one could guarantee that the village would last for long. But it said, in a bold show of support for China's avant-garde, that what it did believe was that real art would last for ever.

THE BANDIT QUEEN

DAVID LOYN DELHI 26 MAY 1994

One of the movies on show at the Cannes Film Festival depicted the life and eventual imprisonment of the notorious bandit Phoolan Devi who, now freed from jail, is planning a life in politics.

Phoolan Devi made her first appearance in public for more than a decade when she stepped from a police van into court earlier this year. The former Bandit Queen is a tiny figure, less than five feet tall, but with a charismatic power. She controlled the police, the crowd and the press more like a politician than a bandit. To the lower castes she's a heroine, and now politicians of low-caste parties are queuing up to exploit her popularity and tap that charisma.

The superintendent of police in Kanpur once spent his life searching for her. He speaks almost wistfully of the days when bandits and robbers worked in the surrounding countryside. Sitting in a police station left over from the days of British rule, he raises his voice above the roar of the air conditioning – it is forty-five degrees outside. There are just two gangs of the old sort operating now, with maybe seven or eight members. Criminals have turned more to kidnapping and drug-running. The robberies of a decade ago, when Phoolan Devi led a gang, seem quaint in comparison. But they were deadly.

In the badlands to the south there is an extraordinary landscape of ravines. Mile after mile of deep trenches with flat dusty tracks at the bottom form a labyrinth where you could hide an army undetected. On St Valentine's Day 1981, Phoolan Devi and more than a dozen of her gang members appeared out of the Chambal ravines and went into a village called Behmai. It hardly even merits the title village, as it consists of just one street of mud houses facing each other. The population numbers less than two hundred, and the people seem to be outnumbered by cows. At the end of the street there's a memorial with more than twenty names on it – men shot dead by Phoolan Devi's gang, who rounded them up and then formed a protective group around her while she carried out most of the shootings. That, at least, is the account of the survivors and the relatives of the dead. In various interviews she has denied that she was there or that she took part in the actual shooting, and the story will never be tested in court. She was released without facing trial after the recently elected Uttar Pradesh state government dropped fifty-five charges. By then she had served more than the eight-year maximum she agreed to when she gave herself up in a highly publicized surrender in 1983: the Supreme Court had no option but to order her release

A lawyer is still trying to bring her to trial, and inevitably there is a strong political element. He's a prominent local member of the BJP, the Hindu Nationalist party, which has lost Uttar Pradesh to the coalition of low-caste parties. The BJP stands for law and order and sees the release as a political gift to use against the new state government. But the low-caste parties want to use Phoolan Devi's popularity among those at the bottom of society. One of their leaders, Kanshi Ram, said recently: 'We have a one-point political programme – for the lower castes to rule India by the end of the century.' The Bandit Queen, for them, is a political asset. When she presided at her sister's wedding last weekend, a state minister was the guest of honour. His bodyguards and the police mixed with former bandits, all carrying guns, but all for the moment on the same side.

The reason why she is seen as such a figurehead of the lower castes is that she says she turned to crime out of revenge for being badly treated by higher-caste men. One account says that she was held and raped over several days by members of the higher Thakur caste, and that the shootings in Behmai were a revenge attack on the Thakurs. In Behmai they deny it. It is true that many of the dead were Thakurs, but there were Muslims and lower-caste people too. They see the attack purely and simply as retaliation because they had informed on the gang to the police.

The old man I spoke to had lost his eighteen-year-old son in the shooting. By chance he had returned to the village only that day to say goodbye after being accepted into the police force. The old man sees the caste revenge theory as sentimental rubbish. He derides the deification of Phoolan Devi, who to him is just a *dacoit*, the word in Indian English for highway robbers and burglars. But there are *dacoit* cults, and Phoolan Devi is seen by some as entering the Hindu pantheon of gods, a demon woman who comes at night to destroy. Other young women have joined the remaining gangs in the Chambal ravines hoping for the fame which attached to Phoolan Devi. And famous she has undoubtedly become. The film, which was first shown at Cannes this week, was described by one excited British critic, Alexander Walker, as focusing world opinion on what he called 'the apartheid of gender and caste' in the subcontinent. He saw it as a celebration of the full force of female empowerment. But that is not how the widows of Behmai see the exploits of Phoolan Devi.

RETURN TO YEAR ZERO

HUMPHREY HAWKESLEY   BATTAMBANG
2 JUNE 1994

*The United Nations hoped their 'model' election in Cambodia
would ensure a calm and democratic future for the country. But
a corrupt military and a resurgent Khmer Rouge rebel force mean
that there is little prospect of lasting peace.*

We were alerted by the squealing of a pig, and pulled up in the dust
along the main east–west highway. A group of children pounded grain
with a stump of wood. A lorry wobbled past, overloaded with people
wrapped in chequered red and white scarves, squashed together with
gun barrels poking out here and there between them. The landscape
was flat. The weather incredibly hot, clear and beautiful, with a haze
which rose off the fields as they stretched away towards the mountains.
Mr Hem Seng was strapping his pig to the back of a bicycle. It was
wriggling, but he was laughing, a cigarette hanging from his lips, as
he fought the animal down and eventually handed it over to a new
owner, who pedalled off to the next village. The price was £15, cash
in hand – insurance money in case he was made homeless. Hem
Seng, who lived in a neat bamboo compound with countless relatives
and children around him, said simply that when the UN had been
running Cambodia last year he had been safe. Now that there had
been elections and the UN had gone, it was dangerous again.

The Khmer Rouge guerrillas were getting closer every day, and he
felt that if he had to flee his village he should have enough money
to look after his family. So although he had never been directly threatened, the shadowy presence of the Khmer Rouge, which hangs over
the whole of Cambodia, had encompassed him. Instead of allowing
his smallholding to flourish, he was selling it off bit by bit in
anticipation of becoming a refugee. He was not over-reacting. Further

up the road, around Battambang, the country's second city, we found 40,000 people camped along the roadside under UN-blue plastic sheeting.

They had fled fighting between the Royal Cambodian Army and the Khmer Rouge, a theatre of battle which stretched almost from the outskirts of Battambang to the guerrillas' headquarters in Pailin, a seedy, gem-mining town on the Thai border. Government troops had captured Pailin, then lost it. The Khmer Rouge had come to within ten miles of Battambang and then retreated. In between were the burnt villages. It is amazing that after being rousted from government in 1979 by invading Vietnamese troops, after being internationally condemned for the mass-murder of its citizens while in power, having signed a peace accord in 1991 and then broken it, the Khmer Rouge are still around. It is as if, after the Second World War surrender, Nazi rebels still held on to large swathes of Germany and were now threatening the government of Chancellor Kohl.

We drove from the roadside refugee camps to the hospital at Battambang and began to piece together a horrific picture of the new democracy in this country. It started with a story about when government troops took Pailin. The senior officers rode into town and daubed the best houses in paint, claiming them as their own. They looted and stockpiled anything of worth: televisions, videos, whisky and cigarettes. They ordered in the best food from across the Thai border.

At the same time, the soldiers who had actually fought the battle were given just one cupful of rice with a pinch of salt for their rations. So when the Khmer Rouge came to take the town back, the soldiers deserted their posts. The officers, of course, ran. One wounded soldier in the hospital said that he had had to make his own way back, because vehicles meant to be used for troops had been commandeered by the generals to ship out their television sets and other booty. Another soldier told how troops shot a colonel who had told them to stand and fight.

A young officer lay dying in the hospital: he had been hit in the head by a hand-grenade. There was no doctor around, and no intensive care, no air-conditioning. His wife had to buy all the medicines he needed, and she said that he hadn't been paid by the government for months. In the brief period that the army held Pailin, the generals had demanded several hundred thousand pounds to repair the road to Battambang, and got it. When the town was lost again, the government asked for the money back – the generals said simply that it had been spent. The war, fought with obsolete equipment by soldiers who do not receive salaries, costs £200,000 a day. It is almost certain that a large proportion of that goes straight into the foreign bank accounts of Cambodia's corrupt military leaders. In other words, if they ended the war they would be doing themselves out of a fortune.

Really, there is nothing more to be said about peace prospects in Cambodia. Most of the people who are running to war on both sides don't want it. The Khmer Rouge earn millions of pounds a year from gem-mining and logging in areas under their control. That wealth would go to the national coffers if there were a peace agreement, and the Khmer Rouge leaders would stand to win nothing. The latest appeal from the Cambodian government is for Western military aid to defeat the Khmer Rouge. That is unlikely to happen. Perhaps the main lesson learned from the £2 million UN operation is that Cambodia has been shown how it should be run; has been given the best chance any corrupt war-torn country is going to get from the international community. The finger of blame has shifted – it is now pointing towards the Cambodians themselves.

DEPARTING THOUGHTS

BRIAN BARRON   HONG KONG   16 JUNE 1994

The BBC's Asia Correspondent left Hong Kong for a new BBC posting in New York. As he packed his bags, he reflected on the humdrum nature of his own move compared to some of the seismic departures he had witnessed in his journalistic career.

It was the Senior Service, with its derring-do, which secured Hong Kong for imperial Britain from an enfeebled China a century and a half ago. Now, with the end almost in sight, the navy and other arms of the British garrison here have been quietly pressing for a starchily proper last act. They would like to strut their stuff, so that the lion exits with an imperial roar and skirl of bagpipes, with departing British helicopters landing on an aircraft carrier, as the People's Liberation Army parades before an apprehensive populace. But in Chris Patten this territory has a working politician as governor. You will not find in his wardrobe the white drill uniform and colonial helmet with ostrich plumes donned by his predecessors.

As commander-in-chief, the governor favours keeping whatever taskforce the Navy can muster over the horizon, while he, perhaps with the Prince of Wales, presides over a distinctly civilian farewell ceremony. Then they would sail from Victoria Harbour on the royal yacht *Britannia*. Military bull would be kept to a minimum, not least because China would probably try to trump anything the British devised. This unpublicized debate is not over yet, but Mr Patten usually gets what he wants in this territory.

On the humdrum level of family departure, we have been counting out the packing cases and dearly hope we count them all in again in Manhattan in the late summer. Possessions have been liquidated, even the baby grand piano, with the promise of a replacement in New York. Once again a couple of battered suitcases are sifted for re-dundant notebooks, maps and audio-tapes from half-forgotten assignments in the 1960s and 1970s to make room for the accumulation of the 1980s and 1990s. But it is an inconclusive struggle; one becomes a hoarder of these crumpled mementoes.

In one file, there is a sheaf of typed scripts from my first British imperial farewell, the humiliating withdrawal from Aden in 1967. Her Majesty's forces limped away as Britain's chosen political successors fled, surrendered or were killed. The British-conceived South Arabian Federation melted into the sand. I watched Colonel Mad Mitch and his Scottish pipers defiantly march out of Crater district and head for embarkation points. A few hours later the revolutionary regime flew in, an unstable cabal of gunmen and guerrilla fighters not much interested in answering questions. Most of those men who, in front of us, first took the reins of power subsequently died by bullet or bomb as the revolution devoured its own children. And even now, in the 1990s, Aden can not escape that dark legacy.

But it is not fair to suggest Britain has any monopoly on messy colonial exits, although Chris Patten's more xenophobic Chinese opponents selectively quote history in making such accusations. Surely the most traumatic and duplicitous withdrawal of modern times was from Saigon nearly twenty years ago. Once again I saw a taskforce assemble – it was the American Seventh Fleet, poised in the South China Sea. For weeks the capital's fate had been sealed as a North Vietnamese armoured blitzkrieg advanced. Planeload by planeload, the Americans pulled out. They abandoned tens of thousands of their counterparts, South Vietnamese compromised by their work in sensitive sectors like information and intelligence. The most poignant sight was the hundreds of Saigonese gathered on the rooftops of office blocks, vainly awaiting promised American evacuation helicopters. They stood there mutely all that last day until the communist tanks smashed down the gates of the presidential palace. Such individuals spent years being re-educated in the jungle prison camps of their northern conquerors.

If confusion and fear are the hallmarks of such enforced departures, nothing prepared us for the chamber of horrors Idi Amin left behind in poor, battered Kampala, the capital of Uganda, when the tyrant and his tribal henchmen were driven out in 1979. We stumbled into the dungeons of the State Research Bureau, the Orwellian name of his secret police headquarters, and found murdered prisoners chained to the walls, steps covered with corpses whose heads had been pulped with sledge-hammers.

On the floors above this charnel-house, in the spookily clean and tidy phone-tapping control centre, sophisticated recorders hummed away at their automated intercepts even though the butchers who controlled them had fled across the Nile. In Idi Amin's palace, there were drawerfuls of bronze medals, including his favourite, the Victoria Cross. A couple of years later, while filming in Idi Amin's home village of Arua, we discovered that the now-exiled dictator had built a massive television station at fantastic cost. But the bush was taking over and the giant satellite dishes were shrouded with creepers, home for green monkeys and exotic birds. It was Africa's answer to the delusions of the former British colonial sergeant-major.

In my business, the point of departure is a stock in trade. One's own hassles and uncertainties on moving, *en famille*, are dwarfed by seismic fiascos witnessed in the recent past. I can't open a suitcase now without recalling Kuwait in the last gasp of the Gulf war. In building after building we found trunks and boxes half-packed with loot stolen by the occupying force of Saddam Hussein – everything from children's toys to chandeliers. It was grand larceny forestalled by the final Allied attack. Just outside Kuwait City, as far as the eye could see, the four-lane motorway leading towards Iraq was choked with immobilized convoys of stolen vehicles, engines still running, which had been cluster-bombed by the Americans. Several contained dead Iraqi soldiers slumped at the wheel. This was retribution on a biblical scale: not so much a military withdrawal, more a getaway that was not. Alongside such folly, the debate in Hong Kong about an unflashy farewell to the British seems eminently civilized.

MR KIM'S BOMB

MARTIN BELL SEOUL 23 JUNE 1994

When North Korea put its troops on a war footing and South Korea prepared for possible nuclear attack, the world wondered just how serious a threat was being posed by North Korea's leader Kim Il Sung.

Just short of the demilitarized zone the lines of trenches and tank-traps stop. The world's most strongly fortified border gives way to a belt of lush vegetation inhabited by egrets and other wildlife, untouched for the present by either war or agriculture. Then up ahead lies the border itself, a clutch of huts surrounded on either side by the grander architecture of peace palaces and pagodas, overlooked at a diplomatic distance by the two largest flagpoles in the world. Flags matter here. The miniature rituals of the border zone matter. The ritual observance of protocol matters. For this is what keeps the two Koreas apart, and at a kind of peace, in the world's last and longest running cold war.

So it was that last weekend, in the politest and iciest of little ceremonies, former American president Jimmy Carter was passed like a package across the demarcation line from one side to the other. The American colonel did not actually sign for him. But, accepting delivery, he gravely thanked the North Koreans for handing him over, so to speak, intact. It was the closest they had been to a dialogue for months. Mr Carter is himself a rare bird of passage: an American who's actually welcome in Pyongyang. Later, in the garden of the American ambassador's bamboo-roofed house in Seoul, he spoke warmly to a sceptical audience of the North Koreans' unique culture, their reverence for their president, Kim Il Sung ('their so-called Great Leader', Mr Carter says carefully), and their national philosophy of self-reliance.

For the South Koreans that is hard to take. The so-called leader is a tyrant, the national philosophy is dictatorship, and the unique culture is the fear and force sustaining the world's last Stalinist regime: not so much a country, more a gulag. More than that, and this is the reason for Mr Carter's diplomacy, the North Koreans are threatening them with nuclear war. The dispute is about Pyongyang's nuclear programme, its evasion of international inspections, its withdrawal from the International Atomic Energy Agency (that really was unique, as unique as its culture). In short, it is a question of whether or not it has The Bomb. It is an issue of the greatest urgency to presidents as well as ex-presidents; in fact, according to Mr Clinton's staff, it is the main foreign policy issue of the moment. For it affects the balance of power in the peninsula and beyond, the Americans' security as well as the South Koreans'. The theory is that the North Koreans, by bluff, deceit and evasion, have extracted enough plutonium from their nuclear programme to make one or two bombs. They have the capability. They have the delivery systems – Scud missiles or even their antique 'Bear' bombers – and they have the determination to make it happen. The South Koreans, with no nuclear programme of their own, are angry and deeply worried. For a moment, before Mr Carter's mediation, a wave of panic swept through shoppers who were buying and stockholders who were selling as if the end were nigh.

The South Koreans' guarantors and protectors, the Americans, are also worried, but less so. The American troops here, a 37,000-strong 'tripwire' force, were practising business as usual. Now the important thing with soldiers – and I think I can speak with some authority here, for I hang out with them a lot – is not what they say, but what they do. And if a commander who has been faced with the threat of invasion by conventional forces believes that has changed to one of nuclear attack, he will change his way of doing things. He will dig. He will retrain. He will assemble, or argue for, a countervailing nuclear force in his side.

But the Americans believe that the bomb, in a deliverable sense, does not exist, or not yet. They know, because they are in the business themselves, that you do not just bolt the device onto the missile. They agree, and are concerned, that the North Koreans have the capability. But they also believe that, to use the jargon of the trade, they have not yet 'weaponized' it. However, this is not to say that they won't. Hence the importance of the present diplomatic push, and of the North Koreans' offer, relayed by Mr Carter, to freeze their nuclear programme while the outstanding issues of inspection and non-proliferation are resolved in face-to-face talks with the Americans. This the Americans will now agree to. It may be unfashionable to speak well of their diplomacy, but the nuclear 'scare' did not actually scare them very much. They are playing a long and patient game, and with reason. The North Korean regime blows hot and cold. It prepares its army, navy and air force for war under guidance of the 'Great Leader'. Just last March it threatened to turn Seoul into a 'Sea of Fire'. But it is caught in its own contradictions: it both seeks and fears contact with the outside world. Its sustaining isolation is also its weakness.

The main event in Pyongyang is Kim Il Sung's official birthday, 15 April. That's when the nation and the world, supposedly, beat a path to the Great Leader's door. Yet at his last birthday, his eighty-second, even that hardy perennial Prince Sihanouk of Cambodia did not show up. Kim had to make do with a former president of Costa Rica, a former Egyptian prime minister, and a bunch of flowers from the Central Committee of the Chinese Communist Party.

So this is the long and patient American view of it: that, yes, North Korea has a nuclear capability. And yes, it can threaten and bluster, and it will. But in the end it is as fierce and as fragile as, say, Ceausescu's Romania. And it will go the same way.

THE KIM IS DEAD, LONG LIVE THE KIM

PHILIP SHORT SEOUL 14 JULY 1994

The death of the man known as the Great Leader, the North Korean dictator President Kim Il Sung, came as the country was poised to enter into crucial talks with the United States. The talks were suspended as the country took part in a massive outpouring of grief. They did start again, but the West remained uneasy about the new man at the top, Kim Il Sung's son Kim Jong Il.

In December 1989, enraged mobs roamed through the streets of the Romanian capital Bucharest, smashing statues of the deposed dictator, Nicolae Ceausescu, and beating to death members of his hated secret police, the Securitate. Ceausescu and his wife, Elena, were court-martialled and summarily shot. North Korea was Romania's closest ally: like Ceausescu, Kim Il Sung had based his regime on an un-bounded personality cult. Also like him, he had placed close relatives in high posts. To Pyongyang, it was an unwelcome reminder of the fragility of autocratic power and the North Korean media system-atically suppressed all mention of the manner of Ceausescu's fall. It is tempting to speculate that Kim Il Sung, as he lay dying after the first of the two heart attacks which ended his life, was haunted by those images of destruction in Bucharest, but that is probably wishful thinking. Ceausescu was, after all, a third-rate petty dictator, an *apparatchik* who took his chance when his predecessor died. Kim, for all the harshness of his rule, the harsh conditions in which North Korean political prisoners were kept and the hermetic isolation of his subjects, was the founder of his country – a man of unquestioned nationalism and extraordinary political subtlety and ruthlessness. So, not surprisingly, it was not the Romanian road that North Korea took this week, but that of China and the Soviet Union.

197

It is all but forgotten now but in 1953, when Stalin died, distraught Russians jammed Red Square, weeping hysterically that the Father of the People, as they called him, had abandoned them. Twenty years later, a million Chinese stood in front of Tiananmen with a similar feeling of having been orphaned when Mao died. The scenes of uncontrollable national grief from Pyongyang over the last few days are in the same tradition. They were of course orchestrated and choreographed by the regime, but they were still rooted in a sense that the one towering figure, around whom every aspect of national life revolved, had suddenly gone – leaving people rudderless and uncertain of the future.

Kim Il Sung may have been a tyrant, but he was the only tyrant most North Koreans had ever known, which is going to make it all the harder for his son, Kim Jong Il, to fill his place. He is fifty-two years old, and has been groomed for power since the early 1970s. North Korean officials say that much of the day-to-day running of the party and state was already in his hands before his father died. Theoretical justification for a dynamic succession, as retailed by North Korean propaganda agencies, was found in the curiously feudalistic idea – which also surfaced in China during the Cultural Revolution – of 'maintaining the revolutionary bloodline'.

The younger Kim has built himself a political constituency in the army and the government, and over the last two decades all those who showed the slightest resistance to his accession to power were systematically purged. Yet the question is whether this short, plump man with the straggling black hair and puffy face, dabbing his eyes with a white handkerchief at the lying in state, will be able to succeed where his father, with all his authority, failed. North Korea faces a dilemma of its own making. If Kim Jong Il tries to preserve the system as it is, the economy will collapse; if he opens the country to bring in foreign investment, it will collapse politically, poisoned by the inflow of foreign ideas – the knowledge, until now rigorously controlled, that the outside world is not the predatory jungle the regime makes it out to be. And whereas, under Kim Il Sung, North Koreans might have been prepared to go on tightening their belts as the country's economic woes intensified, the only way open to his son to establish his political credentials is to provide a better life, and above all, enough to eat, for ordinary citizens. The area of man- oeuvre is desperately small, and no one outside the North Korean inner circle has any real idea of the younger Kim's abilities.

In the West he has been portrayed as erratic and temperamental, responsible for spectacular acts of terrorism like the assassination of half of the South Korean Cabinet in Burma in 1983, and the blowing up of a South Korean airliner, killing everyone on board, four years later. But much of that information comes from the South Korean version of the CIA, which is hardly an unbiased source. North Korean officials say privately that Kim Jong Il is shrewd, but has a quick temper, likes drinking Hennessy and has a huge library of Western video cassettes. He is reclusive, despite a personality cult exceeded only by his father's. Most North Koreans have never even heard his voice. He is also said to be a womanizer, and there are too many stories from diplomats in Pyongyang of leggy blonde Scandinavian girls who claim to have been invited on cultural exchange missions by Kim Jong Il's office for them all to be discounted. However, that does not give much clue as to his political prowess. It is true that he has surrounded himself by technocrats, many of whom are thought to have reformist inclinations; and the decision to resume contacts with the Americans to discuss the resumption of the Geneva talks on, among other things, North Korea's suspected nuclear programme, suggests continuity of policy. But the real tests all lie ahead. Will he have the authority to cut a deal with Mr Clinton, even if he wants to? Will he be able to square the circle, opening the doors enough to breathe life into the economy, yet not enough to destroy the apparatus of thought-control on which the regime depends? All one can be sure of is that North Korea is now an even more unpredictable, uncertain place than it was under Kim Il Sung's idiosyncratic rule.

THE AMERICAS

SLEAZE POLITICS

GAVIN ESLER   WASHINGTON   14 AUGUST 1993

President Clinton, who had swept triumphantly into the White House on a platform promising change, discovered that changes were easy to talk about, harder to deliver.

There's an old Washington joke about laboratory researchers who have given up using rats for experiments and use members of Congress instead. Apparently the researchers never become attached to members of congress, and there are some things that rats just won't do. The joke, in all its many variations, is symptomatic of the disdain with which most Americans view their politicians. Suspicion by the governed of the government was a tradition in the American continent even before the Stars and Stripes replaced the Union Jack, but there is a growing sense among many Americans that government – far from offering solutions – is the principal cause of their problems.

In his book *Government Racket*, Martin Gross lists some of the reasons Americans so dislike Washington. Before the Second World War, for example, Franklin Roosevelt, with the most exciting package of government activism this country has ever known, managed to run the White House with 200 staff. Harry Truman had 285; Jack Kennedy 375. Today the White House has 1,850 employees, and you would be hard-pressed to argue the country is better governed than in 1938 or 1948. Congress is hated even more.

There are 435 members of the House of Representatives and 100 senators, with a total of 20,000 staff. Each House member is allowed eighteen part-time and four full-time aides. In the Roosevelt era it was just two. Each senator now has forty aides, not counting those helping the committees on which he, or occasionally she, might sit. America has yet to make every man a king, but every senator does have a taxpayer-funded royal entourage.

Americans pride themselves on the constitutional separation of church and state, which means that Christian prayers are banned in state schools – but not in Congress. In fact the politicians are so in need of divine counsel that the full-time house chaplain earns £115,000 a year. His senate counterpart – for as with Noah's Ark, American government perks go in two-by-two – earns the same plus a budget of £300,000 a year on top. I am not making this up. Is Congress so wicked that its members cannot even pray without professional assistance? Well, American voters and taxpayers may not know all the details, but they do recognize the smell of stinking fish. That is why 19 per cent voted in the 1992 election for the ultimate outsider, Ross Perot, and why Arkansas governor Bill Clinton is now in the White House.

But the president who promised 'change' and who ran as an outsider has already discovered Washington's central paradox: in order to change anything, a president has to rely on the existing power-brokers, and they have a vested interest in the status quo. That explains, for instance, why the subsidy for honey-bee farmers is contained in Mr Clinton's supposedly radical 1993 budget. In American political biology no plants would be pollinated unless large amounts of dollar bills were stuffed down farmers' throats. The subsidy is exactly the kind of perk that Candidate Clinton so disliked, but which President Clinton had to support to prevent his budget from falling apart in Congress. In Washington, to get along you have to go along.

In fact, the US Department of Agriculture's farm subsidies make the European Community seem a model of efficiency. According to Mr Gross's government waste study, in 1935 the Agriculture Department had 20,000 employees to handle six million farms. Now the number of bureaucrats has tripled, but the number of farmers has dropped to a third. At this rate the one American farmer left in a hundred years' time should have twenty million Department of Agriculture employees processing his request for a subsidy for his honey-bees. The phrase most Americans use is 'pork barrel politics'.

The early pioneers used to salt pork and place it in barrels for winter. The person in charge of handing out the pork therefore had enormous power – and the Prince of Pork today is the West Virginia Senator Robert Byrd, chairman of the Senate Appropriations Committee. His home state is one of the poorest in the country, but thanks to pork power, Senator Byrd has moved government money and jobs to West Virginia: $4.5 million went to renovate an old cinema, for example. The senator wants to shift large slices of the CIA out to his state. He has already succeeded in obtaining a NASA space research centre and the Coastguard's National Computer Operations Centre – which is astonishing when you learn that West Virginia is not even on the sea. The coastguard presumably does not mind.

The White House promised to get rid of the old fashioned pork barrel politics – 'make it Jurassic Pork,' they said. But after his near-death experiences in Congress over the budget, the reformist zeal of President Clinton has been blunted. And perhaps the saddest part of this cynical game came to light with the suicide of Vincent Foster. Mr Foster was the deputy White House counsel – one of the lawyers who advise the president, and a close Clinton friend. Then Vince Foster shot himself and, despite the usual conspiracy theories, the sad truth emerged. The urbane and highly intelligent lawyer from Arkansas just could not stand the pressure-cooker atmosphere of Washington. His suicide note concluded with words most Americans could understand: 'I was not meant for the job or the spotlight of public life in Washington. Here ruining people is considered sport.'

HOW HAITI'S OTHER HALF LIVES

ANDY KERSHAW PORT-AU-PRINCE
11 NOVEMBER 1993

Hundreds of children were reported to be dying in Haiti after sanctions were imposed when the military defied the UN and refused to allow the country's elected president back into the country. Yet it seems there was one group whose lifestyle was unaffected by the difficulties.

The noticeboard at the Petionville Club, in the Hollywood hills of Port-au-Prince, confirms arrival in the Other Haiti's chichi hideaway. Here are adverts for pedigree Irish setter pups, Mercedes jeeps and 'thick gourmet-cut' steaks imported from the United States. Around the swimming pool, Haiti's millionaire mulattos play tennis, sip cocktails and toy with chocolate cake while their children, gathered here for a birthday swimming party, yell for attention in French or American accents before flinging themselves off the springboard. Their parents tut-tut over the US $450 a month school fees.

To gaze out beyond the trim fairways of Haiti's only golf course compounds the sense of the surreal; just a couple of miles below are the rancid slums of the seething capital. Lurking on the horizon is a US navy warship, part of the international fleet sent here to nudge Haiti's military into accepting the return of Father Jean-Bertrand Aristide, the country's first democratically elected president, overthrown in a violent coup in September 1991. The country may be blockaded, but the gateau is being passed around again. For the time being, at least, Port au Prince's MREs (diplomat-speak for Morally Repugnant Elite) are having their cake and eating it too.

Tony, the Jewish-American owner of a beach club forty miles from the capital, says his business is choking because of the fuel embargo. Few of his regulars, lobster-luncheoning officers in the corrupt army among them, can find the petrol to drive out to his weekend playground. 'They daren't buy gas on the black market because we hear it's being watered down and that'll screw up the motor,' he said But the mile-long traffic jam of gleaming four-wheel-drive vehicles I'd just followed up the cratered road from the city suggested full-octane business as usual for those with money. Tony smiled. 'We are all suffering,' he said. 'We all have our little private hells to go through.'

His friend, a middle-aged muscular mulatto in a skimpy posing-pouch that emphasized an implausible bulge, grunted agreement and pushed aside his unfinished cake. A sun-dried white woman at the table flipped the pages of an American fashion magazine and yawned. Fortune-seekers like Tony flourish best without the complications of democracy. Before settling in Haiti, he was summoned to the Dominican Republic by President Rafael Trujillo to organize tourism. Trujillo's assassination in 1961 brought to an end the Caribbean's ugliest dictatorship. Papa Doc Duvalier, by comparison, was a sweetie. Trujillo boiled alive at least one of his political opponents. 'He was just like a grandfather,' Tony recalled.

'We live in a poor country but some people want us all to be poor,' said another club member, a Haitian-born Arab businessman trying to justify the world's most have-and-have-not society. Though his name is not one of those on a US Treasury Department blacklist of coup supporters, many of his friends have had their American assets frozen and visas withdrawn. Unlike them, the Arab businessman is not violently anti-Aristide. Yet for all his gentility, intelligence and generosity he does share the coup-makers' curious interpretation of Aristide's 67 per cent landslide election victory. 'There is democracy and there is legitimacy,' he said. 'Aristide was legitimate but he behaved undemocratically. He wanted to destroy this country and to have it all for himself. You know, all Haitians want to be Duvalier. Every Haitian has that in his heart. Aristide is the same. There were many killings when he was in power.' There were some, though for a country synonymous with the midnight knock on the door by men in dark glasses carrying machine-guns, the Aristide months were the most peaceful in Haiti's history. Americas Watch and the New York-based Lawyers' Committee for Human Rights both praised the priest-president's achievements. Now the streets are crawling again with plain-clothed gunmen, latter-day Tontons Macoutes.

Outside the Bar Normandie, a Macoute stronghold close by the army barracks in downtown Port-au-Prince, I was surrounded by a crowd of two hundred or so drunken thugs. 'Fuck off out of here,' a ragged woman screamed in my face. A youngish guy in a smart blue jacket smiled and beckoned me to his table. 'No photos,' he said calmly, pointing at my shoulder bag. 'Take one photo and I will kill you.' The gunfire around my hotel now starts even before it gets dark. Only during the torrential rains does the shooting stop. Even gunmen don't like to get wet.

The military and the Macoutes have been watching a lot of CNN recently. They know, after the fiasco in Somalia, that the US has no stomach for the invasion to restore democracy that so many poor Haitians were hoping for. Only if they again take to their boats and come swarming up Miami Beach by the thousand, spoiling the backgrounds to the fashion-shoots, would intervention be considered. The Port-au-Prince police chief, Lieutenant-Colonel Michel François, the coup leader, and his nervous frontman, the army commander General Raus Cedras, show no inclination to step aside. President Aristide should have been back in his palace on 30 October. He is still in Washington.

I wondered, by the pool at the Petionville Club, whether Haiti would explode in the coming weeks. 'No,' said the Arab businessman. 'There won't be an explosion here even if the people are starving. They are used to starvation.' Oddly, the impetus for a break in the deadlock and the return of Aristide may come from his natural enemies, the MREs. 'He must come back. This has got to stop,' sighed the Arab businessman. 'The blockade is ruining our businesses. Let him return and we can get on with making money.' Hardest hit by the blockade is the drugs trade. Certain members of both Petionville's élite and the Haitian military have been cited by the US Drug Enforcement Administration for cocaine trafficking. Shipped through Port-au-Prince, Colombian cocaine finds its way to Florida disturbingly smoothly. The DEA puts the profits of the Haitian drug industry at US $200-300 million a year. When he came to office President Aristide targeted the drug barons. Nearly four thousand pounds of cocaine were seized during his seven months in power. The total haul for the year following the coup was precisely zero. Democracy in Haiti carried a huge price-tag.

'The problem with Haiti,' continued the Arab businessman, 'is there are too many Haitians.' Almost a third of the country's six million people live in Port-au-Prince. Particularly during the current rainy season, the wretched inhabitants of the city's slums scramble for an existence in the filth that washes down from cool mountain suburbs like Petionville. The return of democracy will be just the first step towards bringing the two Haitis together. Until that happens, President Aristide's poor and humble masses will go on living right there in the effluent of the affluent.

WAITING FOR THE BIG ONE

STEVE FUTTERMAN   LOS ANGELES
22 JANUARY 1994

Californians live in fear of earthquakes. They know that they live on a fault line, which means frequent small earth tremors and the occasional bigger one. They know that the experts say a huge earthquake, like the one that levelled San Francisco in 1906, is due at any time. So, when our correspondent awoke to find his bedroom shaking, he wondered if the big one had finally arrived.

When you live in California you know the possibility exists: you know that one day you will probably live through an earthquake. You don't necessarily think about it all the time, but you know that one day it's going to happen. Last Monday turned out to be that day. If you have lived in California or other earthquake areas you know the feeling, but you never get used to it. I have been in my share of earthquakes, and while I may not get as frazzled as some people, it's a unique experience. In one sense it is terribly frightening, in another sense it is the most helpless feeling you will ever have, and when the earth finally stops shaking and you realize it's over, there is a feeling of exhilaration. You have survived. Just like millions of other southern Californians, I was asleep when the earthquake began on Monday. It was 4.31 a.m. My first memory is of the room shaking violently up and down – there was no doubt that this was a major quake. I closed my eyes, placed my face in the pillow, and listened as everything in my home went flying around. Books came off the shelves, televisions flew off their stands; it was loud and chaotic. It lasted only around thirty seconds, but they were among the longest thirty seconds I can ever remember. It lasted long enough for me to start thinking such things as: 'Is this the big one?' You can actually see the walls bending and shaking. You wonder if something is going to come down on you – perhaps something on the wall, perhaps the wall itself. When it stops, you slowly open your eyes.

I live in San Fernando Valley, and my home is only around seven miles from the epicentre of the earthquake. So there was quite a bit of commotion. My refrigerator moved about ten feet. The floor looked like a tossed salad of everything I owned: books and paper, mementoes, dishes, compact discs. The sliding doors from a closet came loose and moved down the stairs. It was amazing to see the strange route some of my books took during that bumpy thirty-second ride – one ended up moving about fifteen feet on my top floor, to the stairway, then down the short hallway and into the kitchen. As a correspondent, I have covered my share of natural disasters, but there is something I have always thought particularly frightening about an earthquake. With a hurricane or a tornado, there is always a weather system that gives you some warning. With sophisticated satellite pictures one can actually map out the movements of a storm. With a fire there is usually some time to leave before it engulfs a home. Even with the floods that hit the American Midwest along the Mississippi this past year, most people knew there was danger.

With an earthquake, there is no such luxury. It can happen tomorrow. It can happen next month. It may happen next year – or it may not. The unpredictability of earthquakes was probably best exhibited in October 1989, in San Francisco. Sixty thousand people had gathered inside San Francisco's Candlestick Park to see game three of American baseball's World Series. Tens of millions were watching a live broadcast on television when the shaking began, and suddenly the screen went blank. There had been no hint that an earthquake might happen. Of course, we have all seen the pictures of the destruction it caused: the buildings that crumpled, the apartment complex that collapsed and killed sixteen. But the scene that perhaps best represents the power of an earthquake is the picture of a huge concrete freeway overpass. The overpass is made out of hundreds of tons of concrete and held together by steel reinforcements, but up against the shaking of mother nature, this freeway overpass provided no contest. It was fortunate that the earthquake took place at 4.30 in the morning – if it had occurred during the rush-hour, dozens of cars might have been jammed on the overpass. Perhaps the most sobering news is that this wasn't the so-called Big One, the great quake that scientists say is long overdue.

The last one to hit California was the 1906 San Francisco earthquake. The only thing scientists can say with certainty is that it will happen again; what they can't say is where or when, or how powerful it will be. It could be up to a hundred times stronger than Monday's tremor, and for those of us who lived through that, it is a terrifying thought. It's hard to imagine buildings surviving a quake of such intensity. The death toll is likely to be in the thousands but, as I said at the start, when you live in California you accept the fact that earthquakes are going to take place. You just hope that when they do, you are going to be one of the lucky ones. Most of us were lucky this week.

BILL CLINTON'S STUDENT DAYS

ROBERTA ETTER LITTLE ROCK
3 FEBRUARY 1994

The US president's political ambition was apparent even in his student days, but how true are those stories of sexual shenanigans back in Little Rock, Arkansas? One of his girlfriends tells all.

I remember the bright, moonlit sky that night in Toad Suck Ferry, Arkansas, like it was yesterday. We were sitting in a borrowed car and the last of the country bands were packing away their gear. The sweet smell of honeysuckle hung in the air and the heady feeling of a successful evening was making us slightly giddy. Bill Clinton placed his arm across the back of the car seat and turned to me with a meaningful, but shy, boyish grin. He paused significantly then breathlessly gushed, 'Do you think we have time for one more hot dog?' Our friends in the back seat groaned and tossed a handful of campaign literature up at the windscreen.

That was the summer of 1966, and Bill Clinton was already on the campaign trail – not for himself, but for Judge Frank Holt, who was running for governor of Arkansas that year. We were part of the judge's team of student supporters, not one of us old enough to vote but all hell-bent on changing the world. Travelling in that campaign car with Bill was a real revelation. Everyone had their forged IDs so that we could belch back the odd glass of mountain wine – but not Bill. He never even inhaled the stuff. He was always far happier with a chocolate malt and a large order of fried anything. He also took life on the campaign trail a bit more seriously. While I was collecting off-colour campaign buttons and Janis Joplin records, Bill was collecting people. He kept notebooks with lists of all the people he met; he would then write little notes to help himself remember them and the details of their lives.

It was absolutely fascinating. Bill could walk into a post office in any far-flung backwater town and run into someone he knew. Then it was the pumping of the hand, the clap on the back and 'Say there, Billy Bob. How's it going with that soybean crop? Bag many ducks last week?' To most kids our age he could be an appalling pain, but Bill somehow succeeded in pulling it off with style. I thought he was surely destined either to bore us to death or to lead the world. Mr Squeaky Clean managed to make everyone he came in contact with feel important.

Eventually Bill became governor of Arkansas, which wasn't too much of a surprise to those who had known him. The man definitely had tunnel vision when it came to knowing what he wanted. The funny thing was that he never really changed. He still loved his junk food and had a passion for 'jam sessions' in the kitchen of the governor's mansion, where most Arkansas law was formed. Now, new friends hope to make me feel embarrassed over the so-called sexual peccadilloes of our most famous citizen though, for most Arkansans, it is merely a source of amusement. We 'Arkies' don't even have to thank God for Mississippi any more. Little Rock has finally been placed firmly on the map for Willie Gate and the saga of Bonking Billy.

But the burning question persists. What about those passionate nights of debate in the hot steamy Arkansas summer of 1966? Now that is embarrassing. If the tabloid press is to be believed, I must surely be the only woman in Arkansas not to have sampled those presidential jewels. Last night I phoned my room-mate from the university for our annual New Year's chinwag. My reputation is saved, thank goodness. She, too, had to admit that she had missed the Clinton favours. It seems that there are at least two women in Arkansas who actually slept through Bill Clinton instead of with him.

FIGUERES AND RODRIGUEZ STAND AGAIN

DANIEL SCHWEIMLER   SAN JOSÉ
16 FEBRUARY 1994

Costa Ricans think of their country as a haven of peace and demo-cracy in Central America. While their neighbours, Nicaragua, El Salvador and Panama, have suffered years of dictatorship, revolu-tion and poverty, Costa Rica has enjoyed relative tranquillity. Even the elections take on a carnival atmosphere.

Costa Ricans in general are not a deeply political people. They vote enthusiastically and in large numbers once in every four years, then tend to leave the political élite to get on with it. Three-quarters of all the presidents since 1821 have been descendants of their original colonizers. In the latest elections José Figueres, of the opposition National Liberation Party, won a clear victory. He will take over the presidency in May from Rafael Calderón of the Social Christian Unity Party, whom the constitution prevents from standing a second time. In 1948 Mr Calderón's father, also called Rafael, was president. He was overthrown, in one of the few breaks in the democratic cycle, by Mr Figueres's father, also called José, who claimed that that year's elections had been fraudulent.

Time has moved on, but the names remain the same. This year's presidential campaign was particularly dirty, with both men, José Figueres junior, and the governing party's Miguel Ángel Rodríguez, accusing one another of illegal business deals. Mr Figueres was even accused of being involved in the murder of a drug dealer in the 1970s. Of course, all the allegations were denied, but they left a bitter taste in the mouths of many Costa Ricans. Many thought they were

215

not being presented with a very good choice. But when I asked people if they would abstain they looked at me incredulously. 'No, of course I'm going to vote,' they told me. Thousands returned from abroad, especially from the United States, to cast their ballots and join in the celebrations. Almost every house, car, bus and bicycle waved either the green-and-white flag of Mr Figueres's National Liberation Party or the red and blue of Mr Rodríguez's Social Christian Unity Party.

I made the mistake one day of wearing a green shirt, and was constantly accused of being a National Liberation Party supporter. And voting is not limited to those over eighteen years old. The kids play, too. For the past twenty years a parallel election has been organized for children aged between two and eighteen. More than two hundred thousand took part in this year's election. Separate polling stations were set up, and the children were given the same choice of candidates and went through the same voting procedure. The official candidates even visited the twelve-year-old polling station officials. I was given my press pass by a nine-year-old. The children tend to vote along the same lines as their parents, but I overheard one father scolding his daughter: 'I told you to vote for the green-and-white party' he told her. 'Why don't you ever do as you're told?'

There is no doubt that democracy is thriving in Costa Rica, but problems are mounting and the country is not the paradise the tourist brochures say it is. Costa Ricans think of their country as the Switzerland of the region – peace-loving, democratic and a safe place in which to invest your money. But since its discovery by Christopher Columbus in 1502, not all has been as it has appeared. Even its name – Costa Rica means 'Rich Coast' – came about because of unfounded rumours that vast hoards of gold were to be found there.

Costa Rica has had no official army since 1948, but some of the many strands of the police force wear army-style uniforms and are trained by the military in the United States and Israel. It is a safe place in which to invest, but much of the foreign money now coming into Costa Rica is thought to be connected with the South American drug traffickers who had to find a new place to launder their wealth after the American invasion of neighbouring Panama in 1989. Costa Rica has been opened up to foreign investors, who have been moving in to buy up land and involve themselves in the thriving eco-tourism industry. Public spending has been cut and the impressive health and education systems, built from the proceeds of the country's banana,

coffee and tourist industries, are not what they were. Poverty, unemployment and crime are on the increase.

Much of that seemed to be forgotten during the election party –
presidential candidates always offer a bright future. But the new
president could have a long and difficult four years before the next
elections are celebrated.

SPOOKS, GOONS AND THUGS

PHIL GUNSON SAN CRISTOBAL
12 FEBRUARY 1994

*There are times in a foreign correspondent's life, at any rate in
Latin America, when a journalist's most valuable asset seems to
be the ability to steer a subtle course between naïvety and paranoia.
Our correspondent covering the Zapatista uprising in Mexico
found that if you dropped the naïvety, you were in danger of being
labelled a cynic or, worse, a conspirator.*

Just because you're paranoid, as the saying goes, it does not mean
they are not after you. Mexico, despite its mostly benign international
image, can be an unhealthy place in which to be a journalist – at any
rate, if you are a Mexican. The state of Chiapas, now the scene of a
guerrilla war, is particularly notorious for silencing journalists, through
censorship, false imprisonment and, in extreme cases, even murder. If
a foreigner offends by consistently criticizing those in power, or by
poking a nose into forbidden subjects, the irritation is usually cured
by blackmail or by the application of just enough subtle pressure on
the newspaper or broadcast medium in question, so that the offending
reporter is either withdrawn or gagged. Mexicans can end up dead in
a ditch.

Unusually for Mexico, there is now a huge gathering of foreign
press in the southern city of San Cristobal. They are here to cover
the talks between the government and the Zapatista rebels. This in
turn has led to a huge gathering of assorted spooks, goons and thugs,
here to keep an eye on us. That is in addition to the army, of course,
which has now taken to noting down the names of journalists passing
through checkpoints, their origin, destination and licence-plate

218

number. One young soldier, who was clearly not a specialist in public relations, told us the other day that this new rule was 'so as to be able to control the press better'. Actually, it is the ones out of uniform that scare me. I am not saying that the four men in dark glasses and a white Chevrolet Suburban marked 'press' who cannot remember the name of the newspaper they work for are necessarily spies, any more than the smooth-looking character in a pickup truck with no licence plates who cruised twice around the same block as I was walking to my hotel early one morning, or that nice young man in a sports jacket who somehow turns up reading a newspaper in the foyer of every hotel I check into. Well, I am sure his story of being an English teacher will check out when I get round to investigating him. I suppose I could put down to the defects in the telephone system the fact that every time I start a sentence with a phrase like 'the Mexican army' the line goes dead.

But there is one thing that worries me. The government press centre here hands out credentials, with no photo attached, without ever requiring the alleged journalist to prove his or her identity. By some estimates there are twice as many credentials out there as there are genuine journalists accredited. So not only do we not know who is real and who is not, we are all of us in danger of being mistaken for a false one – which could be really nasty if you are half-way up a mountain in the guerrillas' controlled zones. Not surprisingly, the Zapatistas are taking a dim view of the yellow laminated press cards.

Even more jaundiced is their view of Mexico's television giant, Televisa, which is slavishly pro-government. When the authorities tried to limit the number of journalists who could cover the talks, the guerrillas responded by opening them up to everybody, except Televisa. When I asked a Televisa reporter why he thought they had been excluded, he said some people just did not like their soap operas. The trouble is, I think he was serious. Just like the Televisa journalists, most of the thugs and spooks seem to be working for the government. But like everything else in Mexico at the moment, violence is being privatized. At least part of the government genuinely wants a negotiated solution, or so it seems. But that does not apply to the landowners down in Chiapas, who are desperately afraid of being expropriated to meet the guerrillas' demands. 'What can we do?' one of them lamented the other day. 'The Indians detest us and the politicians won't talk to us.' Well, one thing they can to is to take it out on the journalists. A group from one Mexican newspaper with really distinguished coverage of the conflict, *La Jornada*, was recently beaten up by a fit-looking gang who introduced themselves as the Sons of the Ranchers. So if it is all the same to you, I am going to hang on to my paranoia for the time being. It might just keep me out of a tight spot.

PITCHING FOR
A CHANGE

JEREMY HARRIS   WASHINGTON   30 APRIL 1994

Baseball, the American summer game, is not what it was. The new baseball commissioner has to consider complaints that the sport has become too expensive, that drug-taking among players is rife and that the standard of play is lower than ever. And yet the game continues to exert a powerful hold on the American psyche.

It has been widely reported that Bill Clinton has had trouble filling some senior posts in Washington. Presidential choices for defense secretary, attorney-general and a range of lesser jobs have all proved somewhere between problematic and downright embarrassing. It is not surprising, then, that Mr Clinton has been pondering long and hard on whom to nominate as the new judge presiding over America's powerful Supreme Court. Actually, it seemed at first that the president was going to wrap the whole thing up with uncharacteristic speed. An early and clear front-runner emerged in the form of the Democratic Party leader in the Senate, George Mitchell. But just when it all seemed a foregone conclusion, Senator Mitchell withdrew. Passage by Congress of the president's key health care reforms, he said, must take precedence.

This is a perfectly plausible explanation, but it left millions of American sports fans unconvinced. Many of them believe that Senator Mitchell had a further motive, namely that he really wants to fill another difficult vacancy – that of the country's baseball commissioner. Now, anyone who thinks that running America's favourite summer sport can hardly compare in importance with the epoch-shaping decisions of the Supreme Court is probably right. On the other hand, he or she probably does not understand America. It is not just that the money is much better in baseball – that helps, perhaps, but a Supreme Court justice does have tenure for life, while a baseball commissioner certainly does not. No, it has much more to do with the continuing grip of baseball on the American imagination. It is no coincidence that the Hollywood movie that has come as close as any in recent years to capturing the essence of the American spirit, *Field of Dreams*, was ostensibly about baseball. In a culture where video games and special TV channels have given children a world of their own, baseball still provides a link across the generations. For some American fathers and sons, a summer game of catch with a baseball mitten is fast becoming their only shared pastime.

Ties like that lie at the heart of a remarkable sporting saga, the decision by the greatest player in the history of basketball to pursue a new career in professional baseball. All sorts of motives have been attributed to Michael Jordan's quixotic quest: after all, why would someone who earned an estimated £30 million last year be turning out for a third-grade team in the southern state of Alabama, for £500 a month? The answer, it transpires, is Michael Jordan's father. James Jordan, who was murdered a year ago, was a defining influence on his son. Until the young Jordan started to show remarkable talent on the basketball court, his father hoped he might make the grade in baseball. It is clear from talking to Michael Jordan that baseball is his way of coming to grips with the stunning loss of his father, and of keeping precious memories alive.

In many respects the entire game of baseball has become an uneasy exercise in nostalgia, a kind of precious cultural gem, mined intact from another American age. That nostalgic strain, in a game with a hundred-year history, is evident in a rash of new stadiums. Instead of enclosed, all-purpose concrete sports domes with artificial turf and artificial lighting, the new stadiums are throw-backs to the 1950s and beyond, places of red brick and real turf. Even the advertising hoardings look as though they belong in the Eisenhower rather than the Clinton era.

There is nothing nostalgic, though, about baseball's price-tag. The average salary for a major league player is now over $1,000,000 a year, and top players may get six or seven times that sum. For baseball fans, a trip to the ballgame certainly isn't cheap – a father-and-son outing including seats, a couple of drinks and the mandatory hot dogs and cotton candy can easily cost the equivalent of £60. And it's not just thoroughly modern prices that are worrying baseball purists.

The incidence of drug problems among players is on the rise, hitting and fielding skills are said to be in decline, and some even mourn the replacement by a stick of bubblegum of the plug of chewing tobacco once wedged in a player's cheek. At the same time, support for the game among black Americans of all ages and among teenage Americans of all ethnic backgrounds seems to be in decline. American football and basketball are preferred by the music-video generation, provoking fears that baseball could become a game patronized only by middle-class, middle-aged whites. Relations between owners and players are strained, and few seem sure that the season can be completed without a strike or lock-out. In other words, if baseball is the spirit of an American summer, there are plenty of storm-clouds around. Trying to clear baseball's horizons will present a monumental task for the new baseball commissioner, whenever he's chosen. For now, though, that appointment looks about as trouble-free as the hunt for a new Supreme Court judge.

AN ILL-FITTING HAT

GAVIN ESLER   WASHINGTON   21 MAY 1994

For President Bill Clinton, intervention in foreign conflicts frequently proved disastrous. America's self-esteem was damaged and its relationship with its allies became strained. The president was the global policeman who became increasingly powerless to act overseas.

'Where is George?' He encouraged the crowd to chant as he swung the searchlight trying to spot his rival in the night sky. 'Where is George?' President Bush was leading a trade mission to Japan, but for Pat Buchanan the message was simple. George Bush was minding high-falutin foreign policy, not the bread-and-butter concerns of ordinary Americans. Mr Bush, critics said, was more interested in problems half-way round the world than those half-way down the street.

The beneficiary of Buchanan's political stunt turned out to be Candidate Clinton, whose campaign stuck single-mindedly to the belief that American voters cared about only one thing: 'It's the economy, stupid,' as the sign at Clinton headquarters said. But now for President Clinton the sign has to change. It's Bosnia, stupid. And it's Haiti, stupid. It's North Korea's bombs, and China, Russia, Somalia, Rwanda, Cuba, Iraq, Iran and countless other potential flashpoints, at a time when Mr Clinton appears to be running foreign policy less like a president and more like the governor of Arkansas.

An opinion poll for the *Washington Post* this week showed a sharp decline in confidence in President Clinton's foreign policy. Fifty-three per cent of those questioned said they disapproved of his handling of foreign affairs. Many of these problems – Haiti and Bosnia, for example – are so intractable no quick-fix solution seems possible, and neither the United Nations nor Western Europe seems to hold any better road-map for the way ahead than the White House itself. But Americans, and others around the world, expect America to lead the way. The only real superpower in command, Nato, keeps telling us of the greatest military alliance in the history of the world yet nevertheless manages to look like a pitiful, helpless giant when faced with determined regional bullies.

In Haiti last October a handful of lightly armed supporters of the military regime saw off the USS *Harlan County*, a troopship with 200 US soldiers on board who were supposed to land at Port-au-Prince and retrain Haiti's police. In Somalia, the local warlord Mohamed Aidid led US troops a merry dance and then, after eighteen American personnel had been killed, President Clinton pulled out his forces. In China, the administration threatened to withdraw trade privileges unless Beijing improved its human rights policies, yet everyone expects a fairly weak-kneed compromise.

In April, Mr Clinton on one day held out the prospect of lifting the trade embargo on the Bosnian Serbs. The next day he restated his preference to lift the arms embargo on the Muslims. And the day after that he did neither of those things, instead using Nato on a combat mission that appears to have satisfied no one. Washington Congress, like nature, abhors a vacuum, and into the foreign policy vacuum 435 members of the House of Representatives and 100 senators are now boldly sweeping. Some wanted to invade Haiti and and some did not want to invade Haiti, but above all they want to run American foreign policy if the president will not.

'There is no clarity of policy,' complained the widely respected Republican Senator William Cohen, 'and there is no consistency.' 'Weak and wavering in foreign affairs,' said the *Washington Post*. 'Off course, alternately drifting or steaming in circles, captain rarely on the bridge,' added the San Diego *Union Tribune*. But does any of this matter to the American voters, who may well be satisfied that the economy, stupid, is growing well? Most Americans, despite the incomprehensible Whitewater affair and the embarrassing sexual allegations, really want to like this president, and want him to succeed. And most Americans, beyond their generous humanity which prays for an end to brutality in Rwanda or Bosnia, would find it difficult to put US troops in the firing line in these largely obscure hell-holes.

Yet President Clinton is too astute not to recognize that his failure to establish his authority in the world could eventually prove electorally disastrous. Historians recall that four times this century

Democratic administrations have come unglued over foreign affairs. It happened to Woodrow Wilson in 1920 after the Treaty of Versailles, Truman in 1952 after the loss of China to communism, Johnson in 1968 in Vietnam and Carter in 1980 over Iranian hostages. It could happen to Clinton in 1996 if somehow he squanders America's vast moral and military leadership by failing to exercise the power at his disposal, and failing to match tough rhetoric with action.

It is a case of 'use it or lose it' when it comes to power in Washington, and if Haitian thugs and Somali tribesmen do not take much notice of Clinton's foreign policy, then why should the North Koreans, Saddam Hussein, Iran, Libya or any other potential adversary? 'Our credibility as a world leader is at stake,' moaned the Democratic Senator John Kerry. 'Of all the hats a president wears,' one columnist wrote in *Newsweek*, 'Commander in Chief is still the one that doesn't fit.'

THE NEW SAVIOUR

MARTIN DOWLE   RIO DE JANEIRO   9 JUNE 1994

When our correspondent met the Brazilian World Cup star Romario days before the start of the 1994 tournament, the footballer was in no doubt that Brazil would win and he would be the star performer. He was right: Brazil beat Italy in the final and Romario was the competition's joint top goal-scorer.

To stand on the training pitch of the Brazilian team is like walking on a luscious Wilton carpet soaked in dew. At nine in the morning, the sun is still burning off the early mist, slowly revealing a mountain backdrop that explains why in the last century this was a Mecca for Swiss immigrants. It was in this setting that the national manager, Carlos Alberto Parreira, was wearily explaining his latest riposte to a broadside from the 28-year-old Romario. The Barcelona star had insisted on taking his family to the United States for the World Cup finals, and with his impish grin, Parreira was joking that anyone who wanted to take their families could do so, and their dogs and parrots for that matter.

Suddenly, the media scrum evaporated, and Parreira was left standing alone, an isolated figure in a sea of green. The counter-attraction had finally arrived, fifteen hours late, for an ill-tempered news conference refereed by a harrassed press officer who rapidly ran out of red cards to show to the participants on both sides. In many ways, Romario is as agile with his tongue as he is with his feet. There is no false modesty. Asked what he thought the other members of the selection made of him, he replied: 'They all love me, because they know it'll be me who'll save the team by scoring all the goals.' But at times, the language is less than elegant.

'*E mentira!*' – 'That's a lie!' proved to be the most common answer to questions ranging from his habitual indiscipline to a bizarre rumour that he was due to travel to Argentina that Monday. 'What for?' he snapped. 'Do you think I've got relatives there or something?' Perhaps in a way he has. He is strikingly reminiscent of Maradona, with perhaps a touch of Gascoigne thrown in as well. The angelic good looks can be deceptive. The uncompromising Portuguese of the slums is tempered by a disarming lisp, but that does not stop graphically coarse insults flowing from his mouth. When Pele attacked his indiscipline as unprofessional, he retorted that he would not take criticism from a 'museum piece'.

He swings wildly from incantations about the unity of the team to petulant declarations of independence. In his week back in the country, he turned into a nightmare for the footballing authorities. Instead of reporting for training, he preferred to play 'foot-volleyball' with his pals on the beach, and to go to a late-night rave in the suburbs to the west of Rio, in pursuit of his motto at Barcelona: 'No dancing at night, no goals the next day.' And he threw a spanner into the works after the Varig airline concocted a clever seating plan on the team's specially converted DC10, by insisting on a seat by the window. Varig had proposed seating the players according to their position on the field, which would have meant putting Romario in the very middle, hemmed in by two rival attackers, Muller and Bebeto. Perhaps they should have known that star strikers on a million dollars a year do not take kindly to second-rate seats on aeroplanes.

Brazilian fans are by turns spellbound by his genius on the field, and repelled by his uncompromising behaviour. In a way, he is both a symbol and a reflection of modern-day urban Brazil – chaotic, rebellious, noisy and impervious to laws and regulations. Unlike many footballers of the past who came from poor backgrounds, he never seeks to hide his roots and remains proud of being born in Jacarezinho, one of Rio's least fashionable *favelas*. Like many of his generation, he has thrown off the old habits of deference to the élite and the middle classes, and is not ashamed to portray his indiscipline and coarseness to full public gaze. Nearly ten years ago, at the age of eighteen, he was dropped from a national youth team travelling to Moscow because he made rude signs at the women outside his hotel window. To him, the new order of Rio de Janeiro, with its parallel powers and weak official government, is the natural one. When his father was kidnapped, he did not think twice about contacting the local drug traffickers in the slums to try to retrieve him.

His hate-hate relationship with Parreira stems back to an episode when he flew sixteen hours from Europe, only to be kept on the substitutes' bench. Excluded from the qualifying matches until the crucial game with Uruguay last September, he responded by slamming two goals in the net and saving the bacon of the team and the manager. Now it is clear Parreira needs him more than he needs Parreira. But just to make sure his genius works, an Indian chief from Mato Grosso do Sul arrived in the Brazilian encampment in Santa Clara, California, to ensure good luck for the team. Macsuara Kadiwel prayed for the Brazilian team's victory for the Indians of Brazil and for the native people of all the world. As he put red paint on Romario's face and put his *cocar* or headgear on his head, the Barcelona star was for once stumped for words, though another Brazilian quipped: 'Watch out for John Wayne.'

The ceremony should bring good luck, but it may also spell trouble ahead for Romario. As the self-proclaimed saviour of the team, he knows he has to deliver. On the descent on the road from the training camp in Teresópolis, there is a sign pointing to the 'Grota do Inferno', the cave of hell. Romario may have driven past it too quickly to notice, but therein lie the souls of many footballers who promised much to their country but delivered too little.

FOOTBALL: A MATTER OF LIFE AND DEATH

MARTIN DOWLE BOGOTÁ 19 JUNE 1994

The Colombian football team was eliminated in the early stages of World Cup 1994 after a humiliating defeat by the United States. The reaction at home was furious: the player who had had the misfortune to score an own goal, Andrés Escobar, was murdered days after his return to Colombia. Our correspondent was visiting Bogotá as the Colombian footballers played their first game of a tournament many thought they would go on to win. This one was against Romania. They lost 3:1.

Those who believe that politics should be kept out of sport should give a wide berth to Colombia. Indeed, so great is the confusion between the two, one could almost say that it is sport that should be kept out of politics. Take Colombia's match with Romania, for example. With its team trailing 2:1 at half-time the nation was already, to put it mildly, in a nervous state when the television station announced a newsflash. But instead of being some national calamity, it turned out to be the Liberal candidate with his message to the viewers about the team's performance. Romania, said Ernesto Samper, had pulled some surprises in the first half, but he was confident that the team would still win. 'By what margin?' asked the reporter. 'Three to two,' he declared without a moment's hesitation. Perhaps surprisingly, the Conservative candidate was given no right of reply. But he had his moment too – indeed, many of them, as his commercials appeared at regular intervals during the programme. They consisted largely of shots of Colombia scoring five goals against Argentina in last year's World Cup qualifying game. Occasionally Andrés Pastrana would appear to hold up his five fingers, the margin of victory conveniently coinciding with the number of the Conservative party on the ballot paper. Clearly identifying himself as the underdog, Pastrana argued that beating the team of Maradona showed that favourites could be taken on and defeated – a clear message for his potential supporters. But his Liberal opponent had a rabbit up his sleeve – Colombia's star player, Carlos Valderrama, whose extravagant hairstyle has led to a craze of blond wigs being worn by macho football supporters on the streets of Bogotá. In the Liberal advertisements, Valderrama lends his support to Samper wearing the full national kit. He turns around to show the number ten on the back of his football shirt – you've guessed it, the same number as the Liberal Party on the ballot paper.

In the second half, however, things did not go to plan. Romania slammed in another goal and all Colombia's shots went wide. At this point it was perhaps as well that another category of advert had been appearing on our screens: those dissuading the populace from killing each other after Colombia's matches. This is no joke. In the aftermath of the victory against Argentina twenty-two people died, many from gunshot wounds during the celebrations. One advert says: 'Think about it, we do not want any more football orphans in Colombia.' Another features Valderrama, saying: 'If there is going to be violence, I do not want to be a world champion.' A third features a young Colombian following his national team in a bar in the United States. At the end of the match no one wants to share his emotions and he is left staring into an empty glass. 'Think about it,' says the slogan, 'in Colombia we can all be happy together.' For this opening World Cup match, alcohol sales were banned because it was the eve of the elections and so the traditional street fiesta had not materialized. The streets were deserted; Colombians were feeling disconsolate in their own homes instead. And as it became clear, in the closing moments of the game, that Colombia had no chance of staving off defeat, the sombre president-incumbent, Cesar Gaviria, prepared to address the nation.

Incongruously, since the mood was one of deep depression, cheering Colombians of all races appeared happily singing the national anthem, their eyes gazing upwards. Colourful buses bedecked in the national colours of red, yellow and blue passed in front of our eyes. The presidential broadcast, however, had to vie with mothers phoning up to cry to their children. But President Gaviria soldiered on, accepting the sadness of defeat and asking the nation to have faith, both in the team and in the electoral process. Above all, he wanted to avoid any effect on the next day's voting and any further drop in the turnout, which had plummeted to a mere 33 per cent in the first round.

In the event, he need not have worried; so subdued were Colombians that there was no violence. I asked a Colombian friend why there should be violence and death when Colombia wins and not even a broken window pane when they lose. 'Ah,' he said, 'with us when we win we think ourselves invincible and things get out of control. When we lose we become humble and self-critical.' And thus it was that the next day the voting turnout shot up to 44 per cent and the Liberal candidate was forgiven his off-beam prediction and was duly elected president of the republic.

HEALTH CARE
AMERICAN-STYLE

JON LEYNE   NEW YORK   4 JULY 1994

*The fourth of July is usually thought of as a celebration of all
that is best in the United States. But for our United Nations
Correspondent, who is based in New York, it was the day he was
involved in a car crash which now evokes memories of some of the
worst aspects of the country.*

The casualty department of New York's Bellevue Hospital is more
like a war zone than the peaceful apotheosis of medical science. On
this lively Saturday night, victims of stabbings and gunshot wounds
staggered in to be treated. Up to a dozen police officers tried to keep
order in the mayhem. One particularly violent victim had to be
restrained with leg-irons and handcuffs while the doctors tried to
treat him. A frightening proportion of patients were HIV positive.
For my friends to get treated (I had not been injured) they had to be
strapped rigid to boards for hours in order to protect against aggravating any back or neck injuries – or, to be more precise, to prevent
the hospital being sued for aggravating those injuries. One of my
friends had his wallet strapped to his chest with bandages. Another
had to fight to prevent the medics from tearing up his blazer as they
treated him, as if he was just off the field of battle. And for all of us
there was a long, long wait. After a while I was directed out of this
bedlam to wait for my friends. A strange sight greeted me: patients
were sprawled on the seats of the waiting room, fast asleep. It was as
if they had been waiting there for treatment not for hours or days,
but for years. Then I realized that these were not prospective patients
– this was where the homeless of New York spent the night.
   I've had a lot of experience of American medical care since then,

and I fear that my first surreal impression was all too accurate. This
is a bizarre, haphazard system mixing excellence with awfulness.
Nobody is actually left lying on the street after a road accident, but
the subsequent quality of care varies widely. 'What insurance do you
have?' they keep asking you. If it is good enough you progress up to
the next level of care, if not, then who knows ... The aftermath of
one visit I made to hospital for an injured knee has been an endless
cascade of paperwork, still arriving months after the treatment: bills
for the X-ray, bills for the medical technicians' time, bills for the
doctors, bills for the use of the hospital. I think that I have notched
up nearly $2,000 in bills for that one injury alone. It is the best
treatment in the world – if you can afford it. I am not qualified to
judge its quality, but I do know that health care in the United States
is money-motivated in a way almost unknown in Britain. I heard one
doctor almost shriek with horror when his receptionist innocently
asked whether he had agreed to treat a patient for free. Have enough
insurance, and they fall over themselves to treat you; too little, and
you can forget it.

As President Clinton pointed out recently, the United States spends
a vast part of its wealth on health care – more than twice as much
as Britain, as a proportion of its gross national product. Yet there is
still no guarantee of universal cover. Even some middle-class professionals I know in New York cannot afford insurance, and cannot
get treated for some conditions. It is a strange situation for a nation
which usually values its creature comforts so highly. America seems
to have a mental block about health care, just as it does about those
lethal taxis.

Back in the Bellevue Hospital, I did not have to sleep the night
with New York's homeless. As a 'respectable' citizen I was allowed to
lie on the couch in the lobby, alongside the bureau offering no doubt
much-needed financial loans, and under the watchful eyes of the
vigilante Guardian Angels. But there was a wake-up call at 7 a.m. for
all of us, whether or not we had homes to go to. The homeless
dutifully got up and resumed their patrol of the streets. The emergency room finally finished the routine check-up on my friends
more than eight hours, one long night, after they had been admitted.
We decided to walk home this time, rather than risk another ride in
a yellow cab. And that was my first experience of the fourth of July.

THE CRACK BABIES OF CHICAGO

BRIDGET KENDALL WASHINGTON
14 JULY 1994

The scale of the drug problem in the inner cities of the United States is far greater than that in the equivalent British cities. Although British doctors expressed concern about the number of babies being born already addicted to crack cocaine, it was clear that the problem was more severe in American cities such as Chicago.

Thirty-year-old Catina smoothed her dungarees over her curved stomach. 'My due date is December,' she said in a soft drawl. 'My drug of choice was marijuana laced with cocaine. I came here when I was three weeks pregnant. I need to come off drugs for my baby's sake.' I had expected the addict mothers of cocaine babies at this drug treatment centre to be withdrawn, hard to talk to, even suspicious. Catina instantly put me right. She might be black and from a poor area of Chicago, but she was bright, articulate and had a degree in business administration. She used to work for a large consultancy firm, and would get high in the lunch-hour like many of her friends working downtown.

Trina is twenty-five years old; she, too, used to have a good job, as a secretary. She is white and grew up in a quiet Chicago suburb. She first got into smoking crack, the particularly addictive cocaine derivative, when she was pushed into it by the father of her second child. Trina had the strength of character to try to kick the habit. Then she gave birth to a third child, and on the same day her mother died after nine painful months of cancer. Trina could not cope: she turned back to crack.

Weaving in and out of these women's life stories was a pattern of violence and death that led to despair. Shana, twenty-three years old, is sweet-faced and cheerful: 'I've had three children,' she said, 'and the baby in my stomach makes four.' But then, in a matter-of-fact way, her story well-rehearsed from hours of drug treatment therapy, she explained how she had lost her two-year-old son, André. She had left him with her sister and her husband while she went off in search of crack; when she came back the brother-in-law had beaten the toddler to death. The pain and the hurting, she said, just took her into drugs deeper, because there was nowhere else to go.

Some talked of reaching the bottom – like Leonore, gentle, serene and, at thirty-two, the mother of six children. 'I'm just a struggling young black woman trying to survive,' she recited with a smile. But then she recalled how she used to drink and smoke drugs; all she had wanted was to die. 'My baby's father used to beat me real bad,' she explained. 'Once he cut open my eye. I was unconscious. I woke up in the ambulance; they were shouting that my heart had stopped. Then they asked me the names of my chilren, and for the first time I prayed to God not to let me die.'

It was hard, sometimes, in these conversations, to work out which came first. Was it the family violence that pushed a woman into drug addiction, or did the brutal battering happen because man and wife were out of control on drugs or drink? Or did the therapy sessions at this well-meaning treatment centre encourage these women to look for childhood abuse, or family tensions, to explain their need to lose their mind for a drug high?

Most thought-provoking of all, though, was the story of Vanessa. I went with a welfare worker to pick her up from the dilapidated tenement block where she lived. The worst thing, she told me, as she sat in the van, eating her breakfast of fried chicken and grits, was to have teenage sons. She had two, currently in state custody while she tried to deal with her addiction. 'But there is no way you can keep them safe,' she said. 'You just go out on your front porch, and those drug dealers try to trap you, promising the kids $200 training shoes if they will run across the street with a package of cocaine. I save up $5 from my welfare cheque to give my boys on a Saturday, and there is no way I can compete. It is worrying about my boys that started me on drugs.' The motivation for dealers is strong. Children do not usually get put in prison. If they are caught, the drug dealers sit outside the county jailhouse in their vans, waiting for the kids to come out, so they can put them back to work again.

The scale of this drug problem makes a solution hard even to imagine. One doctor in charge of an intensive care unit full of premature crack babies admitted that he did not believe in what he was doing. Taking babies away from their mothers if they tested drug positive was no good, he said; it did not even curb the flow. The cost of finding foster care for babies in Illinois this year will be $1 billion. Added to that there is the risk of traumatizing the baby, while you drive the mother further into despair, or worse still relieve her of her responsibilities so she can prostitute herself again to pay for more cocaine and produce another infant, who next year will be yet one more baby for the state to place in foster care. In some cases, like those of Catina and Leonore, it is true the mother may reach the end of her tether and seek treatment so that she can get her children back. But is there not a risk that the children then become currency, a sort of prize awarded to a mother if she behaves well?

What, after all, is going to happen to Catina, Leonore and Shana when they finish their eighteen-month course of treatment and have to find somewhere to live and a job to support themselves and their new babies? The lesson they are being taught is to cut themselves off from their old world, even if that means husbands, brothers, even mothers, who might entice them back to old habits. So where else do they go? How do they avoid the preying dealers hanging around the street corners, whispering as they go past? Ask any of these young women, and their smile will disappear, their face will cloud over. 'Well I'd like to get a job in the social services,' they say anxiously. 'I'd like to stay here. Maybe I could get a job filing in reception or become a drug counsellor.' Some even admit what others are too scared to say: return to Chicago's south side, and how do you resist the culture of guns and drugs and hope to survive?

HAITIAN HIATUS

CHRIS WEST   PORT-AU-PRINCE   28 JULY 1994

A fleet of American warships lay off Haiti as the United Nations debated whether to authorize an American-led invasion to restore to power the country's elected leader, Jean-Bertrand Aristide. But as Haiti waited to see what would happen, its people carried on living as usual – in fear and poverty.

In this land of voodoo and spells, it is all too easy to believe an illusion. Driving through the northern mountains, through lush velvet green valleys and orderly villages, I saw thoughtful-looking men in white shirts and ties ambling through the streets, clutching Bibles. Pretty young girls in frocks of pink and blue chattered happily as they made their way to church. Was this the island, I wondered, where a fleet of American warships lay just over the horizon, ready to move in to restore order? The illusion evaporated as I emerged from this lost valley onto the plain denuded of its trees by the short-sightedness of successive regimes, and on towards the capital, Port-au-Prince. The road, a hundred kilometres of it, is little more than a lattice of concrete shot through with pot-holes which can, and do, break a car's back in seconds. I had been told that the sad state of the road was the work of a corrupt engineering department which had done a spectacularly botched job. I was soon put right by the man at the Information Ministry: the pot-holes, he said, were the work of communists.

In the two hours while I waited for an audience with the minister, he told me how his son wanted to travel the world but, alas, could not do so because of the international embargo imposed on the Haitian regime. His youngest children were unable to go to school because the sanctions meant there was no petrol for the family car. The communists, led by public enemy number one, the ousted

President Aristide, had a lot to answer for. What would he do if American troops got the green light from the UN and stormed in? He rose from behind his desk, threw open the neck of his shirt, and declared with a passion worthy of Gielgud: 'I will be there with my wife and baby – they will have to shoot us all.'

That particular functionary's explanation of Haiti's woes can be given the lie with a brief visit a mile or so down the road to the shanty town named, by someone with a exaggeratedly cruel sense of the absurd, Cité Soleil. It means Sun City, but there are parts of this fetid, disease-impregnated slum where you despair of the sun ever shining. The people who exist here are paying the price for their support of Aristide. It is here that the death squads find most of their victims, leaving them mutilated in full view as a warning to anyone who feels like stepping out of the government line. Seventy per cent of the country is below the poverty level, but that is an average – in Cité Soleil, poverty would be a luxury. There is a bright, almost jaunty, young man called Johnny who will show you around, not that you need much guiding to see the heaps of steaming, rotting refuse or smell the stench of the overflowing open sewers. Johnny is one of the few who dare to speak openly. He will talk at length in good, American-accented English of his hatred for the military regime. I only hope that Johnny is around for a long time to come: while he introduced me to people in the meeting places between the tumble-down shacks, two well-dressed men approached us. I did not need a command of Creole to understand their advice – that Johnny's time might be more profitably spent doing something else.

That is another of the mysteries of Haiti: for a police state, it seems to have very few police. But make no mistake, they are there, usually in the form of sinister government 'attachés', or the thugs of the ultra-right-wing group FRAPH, whose greatest joy would be to return to the days of Papa Doc or Baby Doc Duvalier. Their leader denies that his men are behind the death-squads: 'But we have to use muscle, the Haitian people are like children,' he says.

The desperate inhabitants of Cité Soleil chant Aristide's name like a charm, but there is no real enthusiasm in their eyes. Anyone who could improve their squalid existence would get their vote. One charming and educated man whom I met in Port-au-Prince told me he had voted for this priest-turned-politician less out of conviction than in the last-ditch hope that almost anyone new could make things better. Certainly President Aristide's credentials before he was ousted in 1991 did little to endear him to whole sections of Haitian society, whose support, however muted, might have allowed him to cling to power. In his short time in power he managed to alienate everyone, from the army to the legislature. Even after exile in Washington he continued to demonstrate that conciliation is not one of his strong points by declaring that he would refuse to return to Haiti with the connivance of the hated Americans. He has softened his line since.

The man who overthrew him is, on the surface, an archetypal Latin American dictator. General Raoul Cedras, according to gossip in Port-au-Prince, did not really want to lead a coup against the man who appointed him, but his name was put forward and the buck stopped right there. There are tales of disagreements between him and colleagues, and it is even being said that he might be prepared to leave Haiti for a financial consideration and a safe haven. But the party line remains upbeat: 'We're surviving sanctions, we can take an invasion in our stride!'

UN approval for armed intervention may concentrate the general's mind, but it does raise the bizarre spectre of Washington battling a right-wing regime to install a nationalist and socialist who might well express his gratitude by shunning the United States once he is back in power. But the vile excesses of the Cedras regime are too much even for CIA hardliners, who shudder at the thought of Jean-Bertrand Aristide in their backyard. It is not a pretty dilemma for the USA, where opinion polls maintain that nothing that happens here is worth a single American life. In Haiti, no politician worth his salt would make an important move without first consulting a voodoo priest. It may be advisable for Bill Clinton to do likewise.

CONTRIBUTORS

Paul Adams   Reports for the BBC from the Balkans
Brian Barron   BBC New York Correspondent, formerly based in Hong Kong
Meriel Beattie   Reports for the BBC from Eastern Europe
Martin Bell   BBC Foreign Affairs Correspondent
Jeremy Bowen   BBC Foreign Affairs Correspondent
Julian Borger   Reports for the BBC from Eastern Europe
Malcolm Brabant   BBC Athens Correspondent, also reports from Bosnia
Alex Brodie   BBC Middle East Correspondent
Simon Calder   Travel writer and broadcaster
Tom Carver   Reports for the BBC from South Africa
Kevin Connolly   BBC Paris Correspondent, formerly based in Moscow
Martin Dowle   Reports for the BBC from Central and South America
Mark Doyle   Reports for the BBC from Africa
Gavin Esler   BBC Chief North America Correspondent
Roberta Etter   Travel writer and broadcaster
Matt Frei   BBC Southern Europe Correspondent
Steve Futterman   Reports for the BBC from the United States
Misha Glenny   Author and former BBC Central Europe Correspondent
Peter Godwin   Reports for the BBC's *Assignment* and *Panorama* programmes
Chris Gunness   Reports for the BBC from the Far East
Phil Gunson   Reports for the BBC from Central and South America
Bill Hamilton   BBC Correspondent
Jeremy Harris   BBC Washington Correspondent
Humphrey Hawkesley   BBC Beijing Correspondent, formerly based in Hong Kong

Roger Hearing	BBC East Africa Correspondent
Alfred Hermida	BBC North Africa Correspondent
Lindsey Hilsum	Reports for the BBC from Africa
William Horsley	BBC Bonn Correspondent
Simon Ingram	BBC Cairo Correspondent
Stephen Jessel	Former BBC Paris Correspondent
Fergal Keane	BBC Asia Correspondent, formerly based in South Africa
Bridget Kendall	BBC Washington Correspondent, formerly based in Moscow
Andy Kershaw	Writer and broadcaster
Jon Leyne	BBC United Nations Correspondent
Allan Little	BBC Correspondent
Tim Llewellyn	Former BBC Middle East Correspondent
David Loyn	BBC South Asia Correspondent
Tim Luard	Reports for the BBC on the Far East
James Miles	Former BBC Beijing Correspondent
Paul Reynolds	BBC Diplomatic Correspondent
Stephen Sackur	BBC Middle East Correspondent
Tim Sebastian	Author and former BBC Eastern Europe Correspondent
Daniel Schweimler	Reports for the BBC from Central and South America
Philip Short	BBC Far East Correspondent
John Simpson	BBC Foreign Affairs Editor
Chris West	BBC Correspondent
Tim Whewell	Former BBC Moscow Correspondent
Monica Whitlock	Reports for the BBC from Iran
Nigel Wrench	Reports for the BBC's *PM* programme